DATE DUE

IT HAPPENED TO ME

Series Editor: Arlene Hirschfelder

Books in the It Happened to Me series are designed for inquisitive teens digging for answers about certain illnesses, social issues, or lifestyle interests. Whether you are deep into your teen years or just entering them, these books are gold mines of up-to-date information, riveting teen views, and great visuals to help you figure out stuff. Besides special boxes highlighting singular facts, each book is enhanced with the latest reading lists, websites, and an index. Perfect for browsing, there are loads of expert information by acclaimed writers to help parents, guardians, and librarians understand teen illness, tough situations, and lifestyle choices.

1. *Epilepsy: The Ultimate Teen Guide,* by Kathlyn Gay and Sean McGarrahan, 2002.
2. *Stress Relief: The Ultimate Teen Guide,* by Mark Powell, 2002.
3. *Learning Disabilities: The Ultimate Teen Guide,* by Penny Hutchins Paquette and Cheryl Gerson Tuttle, 2003.
4. *Making Sexual Decisions: The Ultimate Teen Guide,* by L. Kris Gowen, 2003.
5. *Asthma: The Ultimate Teen Guide,* by Penny Hutchins Paquette, 2003.
6. *Cultural Diversity—Conflicts and Challenges: The Ultimate Teen Guide,* by Kathlyn Gay, 2003.
7. *Diabetes: The Ultimate Teen Guide,* by Katherine J. Moran, 2004.
8. *When Will I Stop Hurting? Teens, Loss, and Grief: The Ultimate Teen Guide to Dealing with Grief,* by Ed Myers, 2004.
9. *Volunteering: The Ultimate Teen Guide,* by Kathlyn Gay, 2004.
10. *Organ Transplants—A Survival Guide for the Entire Family: The Ultimate Teen Guide,* by Tina P. Schwartz, 2005.

LIVING GREEN

THE ULTIMATE TEEN GUIDE

KATHLYN GAY

IT HAPPENED TO ME, NO. 31

THE SCARECROW PRESS, INC.
Lanham • Toronto • Plymouth, UK
2012

Published by Scarecrow Press, Inc.
A wholly owned subsidiary of The Rowman & Littlefield Publishing Group, Inc.
4501 Forbes Boulevard, Suite 200, Lanham, Maryland 20706
http://www.scarecrowpress.com

10 Thornbury Road, Plymouth PL6 7PP, United Kingdom

British Library Cataloguing in Publication Information Available

Library of Congress Cataloging-in-Publication Data

Gay, Kathlyn.
 Living green : the ultimate teen guide / Kathlyn Gay.
    p. cm. — (It happened to me ; no. 31)
 Includes bibliographical references and index.
 ISBN 978-0-8108-7701-6 (hardcover : alk. paper) — ISBN 978-0-8108-7702-3 (ebook)
 1. Sustainable development. 2. Environmental responsibility. 3. Green movement. I. Title.
 HC79.E5G3529 2012
 338.9'27—dc23   2011040607

∞™ The paper used in this publication meets the minimum requirements of American National
Standard for Information Sciences—Permanence of Paper for Printed Library Materials, ANSI/
NISO Z39.48-1992.

Printed in the United States of America

Contents

INTRODUCTION: LIVING GREEN—WHAT DOES IT MEAN?

Being eco-conscious "is who I am and how I live. . . .
Sometimes I think I live in this little green bubble, but I really believe in it."
—Erin Schrode, New York University student[1]

Green your school. Green your home. Green your lunch. Green your dorm room. Green your prom. Green your gift packaging. Green your cosmetics. Green your clothing. Green your cleaning supplies. Green your social networking. Green your grocery shopping. Green your vehicle. The word *green* has become a verb, as well as an adjective and the name of a color, and it is being used in many advertising messages promoting green products and services that are supposed to be eco-friendly—that is, those products that help consumers young and old to live green and protect the environment.

Until recent decades, the living green idea was not a widespread concept in the United States, although many Americans were concerned about environmental pollution and conserving natural resources. During the 1950s, for example, people "lived green" because that was the way things were done. Glass bottles were regularly returned to a store or plant to be washed, sterilized, and refilled. Parents washed cloth diapers and hung them on a clothesline or rack to dry for reuse. Most lawns were mowed with a push mower that did not emit pollutants. Worn work clothes were patched for reuse. When children outgrew their jeans, dresses, coats, or other attire, the clothing was handed down to younger siblings in a family. Planting a garden or buying fresh produce from a local farmer was a common activity in the suburbs.

Using Green as Symbols

Because the color green is associated with nature and growing things like grass and shrubs, green is now related to environmentally friendly goods and services. Of course, there is a flip side. What if a person is "green with envy"? The term also is associated with greed and the accumulation of a lot of "greenbacks." And being a "greenhorn"—someone who is a novice—usually is not meant as a compliment. Nevertheless, green also symbolizes growth, so a novice gardener, for example, could certainly grow in experience and maybe develop a "green thumb." In addition, green is the color of the four-leaf clover, a good-luck symbol and a traditional part of St. Patrick's Day celebrations. On the quiet side, green is considered a restful color, and some people believe it relieves eye stress. Then there is the green olive branch that is regarded as a peace symbol. And in Asia, green jade is a sacred gem; in China it is called the "Stone of Heaven."

In contrast, current magazines and newspapers publish numerous articles that tell readers how to recycle bottles, paper, clothing, and other items; reduce consumption of goods and energy use; buy locally to save energy; use eco-friendly products; and so on. Books provide page after page of green living ideas. Television shows and websites feature "tips" for living green. But the question remains: What does living green today really mean?

What People Say about Living Green

According to the website *Green Living Tips and Ideas*, "Living green means different things to different people. However, one common theme persists despite these differences in opinion—living green means making the choice to lead lives aimed at achieving health for one's self, for one's community, and for one's environment. In short, it is the conscious choice to be more eco-friendly, day in and day out."[2]

Teenager JordAn Howard of Los Angeles, who is leader in a program called Green Ambassadors, encourages her peers to "start small, with simple changes, whether it be [switching to] fluorescent lightbulbs or turning off the water when you brush your teeth. And that change will build, and you'll want to do more. That's what I did. Don't just be the change. Teach other people."[3]

At Highlands High School, San Antonio, Texas, student Jonathan Regaldo petitioned to have solar panels installed in his school. According to a report by Eva Gonzalez, a junior at Highlands, "He believes that if the high school sets an example to the community then it will follow. The response to his petition from students and teachers has been remarkable. . . . He has received the principal's approval . . . [and] looks forward to receiving the district's authorization. Later on . . . he hopes to attend the Green Apple Festival where he would do renovations like planting trees in Austin."[4]

In Boulder, Colorado, students at New Vista High School also have gotten permission to install solar panels on the roof of their school. This is just one example that students hope will help others in the community become aware of options to protect the environment. One student, Zander Deetz, "brings a lunch to school that mainly consists of local food, only eats meat occasionally because of the energy it takes to produce and bikes to school (weather permitting). He also encourages others to live sustainably."[5]

Lubbock, Texas, teen Chance Bretz notes: "I believe in going green because I like to recycle, it's good for the environment. We are filling the world with so many toxins and pollution, it's the least we can do." One of his peers, Eddie Bohannon, adds, "Recycling is good for the environment. I pick up cans off the side of the roads and recycle them. I do it for money, but I know it also cleans up the environment."[6]

For teenagers (and adults) in other parts of the United States, living green means reducing their impact on the planet—changing their lifestyle to produce less waste. It means abiding by such principles as reducing consumption, waste, and pollution and conserving energy and natural resources. Underscoring these general concepts is this basic premise: Protect the ecological balance on earth so that humans and other beings can sustain life.

What Sustainability and Biodiversity Mean

Sustainability is a key word when discussing what it means to live green. When thinking about one of our basic needs—food—agriculture experts say that

> sustainability rests on the principle that we must meet the needs of the present without compromising the ability of future generations to meet their own needs. Therefore, *stewardship of both natural and human resources* is of prime importance. Stewardship of human resources includes consideration of social responsibilities such as working and living conditions of laborers, the needs of rural communities, and consumer health and safety both in the present and the future. Stewardship of land and natural resources involves maintaining or enhancing this vital resource base for the long term.[7]

Food growers and producers who engage in sustainable agricultural practices balance the long-term environmental effects of their farming or ranching practices. They might protect groundwater and streams from livestock waste and agricultural chemicals, for example. They might use integrated pest management (IPM), which involves using a pest's natural enemies, such as adult lady beetles (or ladybugs) and their larvae (insects in their wormlike stage), because they feed on lice that kill plants, instead of chemical pesticides. In some cases, the IPM strategy might be to simply harvest a crop before harmful insects can cause damage. Another sustainable practice is rotating crops—planting different crops in a field during growing seasons so that the same crop each year does not deplete the soil or get wiped out by pests.

Sustaining the earth's natural resources goes hand in hand with preserving biodiversity—that is, maintaining the biological diversity of animal and plant species. What is so important about biodiversity? For one thing, animals and plants are food sources, and when only one species of a crop is grown, pests or natural disasters can destroy that crop. With biodiversity an alternative food source would be available. Preserving biodiversity also helps ensure the protection of the plants and animals from which medicines, fertilizers, and pesticides are derived.

Many people believe that sustainable practices are the responsibility of government and big corporations involved in agriculture, forestry, fishing, manufacturing, mining, transportation, and other industrial endeavors. But each of us plays a role in sustainable (or green) living by being aware about one's lifestyle. In short, there are options in what a person consumes and throws away and how each of us conserves and protects the environment.

Teen Activists Are Everywhere

As people of all ages become increasingly aware of what it means to live green, young people across the United States forge ahead with their own ideas for environmental protection. Some teenagers were prompted to take action after the 2010 catastrophic oil spill in the Gulf of Mexico. For example, teenager Matt Pierce of Bradenton, Florida, started a nonprofit called Teenagers Care to raise funds to help save beaches and animals suffering from the disaster. His idea spread so quickly that in less than two weeks the organization raised almost $5,000 and continued to raise even more.[8]

At a Kalamazoo, Michigan, high school, students have formed an environmental club. Several club members said they walk or ride bikes to school to save energy and cut down on pollutants from vehicles that contribute to global warming.

In St. Petersburg, Florida, high school student Evie Sobczak conducted an experiment to create an alternative fuel—a fuel made from plants, animal fats, garbage, or a source other than nonrenewable fossil fuels. In her experiment, which won a first-place award at a science fair, Evie created fuel from algae, a plant that reproduces quickly. Evie hopes in the future to work within the "area of renewable energies and resources because that's really the way our whole world is going to go when we run out of fossil fuels."[9]

Projects to save manatees, dolphins, seals, whales, and other types of animals engage numerous teenagers. For example, since 2001 teenager Alexandra Weinstein of Essex, Massachusetts, has been speaking out about the inhumane slaughter of thousands of whales for their meat and oil and has held "Save the Whales" parties to call attention to the issue. Teenager Stephanie Cohen, a member of the Student Advisory Council of the Humane Society of the United States, began Kids Making a Difference (KMAD) in 2003. This award-winning, nonprofit organization "brings youth who have a common interest in helping animals together in order to have a positive influence on the world in which we live."[10]

In urban areas and on reservations in the United States, teens also are involved in efforts to stop dumping of toxic trash in or near their communities where people have little power to prevent the poisoning of their environment. Young people are part of river, park, and beach restoration efforts. Nineteen-year-old Samantha Koral, for example, says she "cleans beaches twice a year in [her] hometown [of] Malibu, California."[11] In many parts of the United States, teenagers make an effort to eat foods that are grown locally. They advise that eating locally cuts down on transportation and saves energy. Other programs for living green include student school projects and efforts to make homes more eco-friendly. And recycling is one of the most common teen endeavors. This book explores teen involvement and their views about being green.

Notes

1. Stacey Palevsky, "Eco-Teen Awarded $36,000 Diller Tikkun Olam Award," August 13, 2009, www.jweekly.com/article/full/39556/eco-teen-awarded-36000-diller-tikkun-olam-award (accessed May 1, 2011).
2. "What Does Living Green Mean?" *Green Living Tips and Ideas*, September 10, 2010, www.getgreenliving.com/what-does-living-green-mean (accessed August 13, 2011).
3. Current Events. "Green Teen." *cenewsblog.com*, April 22, 2009, www.cenewsblog.com/main_news/2009/04/green-teen.html (accessed April 14, 2011).
4. See *Teen Team Blog*, "Teen Talk, No. 3: In Appreciation of Steward of the Earth," April 4,

2009, http://blog.mysanantonio.com/teenteam/2009/04/teen-talk-no-3-in-appreciation-of-stewards-of-the-earth (accessed April 18, 2011).

5. Marisa McNatt, "Teens Say 'Environment' Is Top Concern," *earth911.com*, February 25, 2010, http://earth911.com/news/2010/02/25/teens-say-environment-is-a-top-concern/#comments (accessed April 18, 2011).

6. Quoted in Laci Talerico, "Teenwise: Teens Going Green," *lubbockonline*, April 26, 2009, http://lubbockonline.com/stories/042609/fea_432996099.shtml (accessed August 18, 2011).

7. University of California Sustainable Agriculture Research and Education Program, "What Is Sustainable Agriculture?" December 1997, www.sarep.ucdavis.edu/concept.htm (accessed May 23, 2009).

8. "Mathew Pierce," www.humaneteen.org/?q=node/ 1318 (accessed May 1, 2011).

9. Quoted in Carly Hart, "Shorecrest Prep Student Wins Pinellas Science Awards for Biodiesel Fuel Research," *St. Petersburg Times*, April 19, 2011, www.tampabay.com/news/human interest/shorecrest-prep-student-wins-pinellas-science-awards-for-biodiesel-fuel/1164692 (accessed July 14, 2011).

10. Stephanie Cohen, The Humane Society of the United States, January 28, 2011, www.humane society.org/about/departments/students/student_voices/advisory_board/stephanie_cohen. html (accessed July 16, 2011).

11. Samantha Koral, response to author questionnaire, May 19, 2010.

CARING FOR THE EARTH

··

"The earth is being destroyed and we're not doing anything."
—teenager Nate Pahe of the Washoe tribe[1]

The early caretakers of the environment in the Americas were indigenous people. Tribal groups who first inhabited the continent were well aware that all life on earth is interconnected and that Mother Earth needed protection. On the other hand, European colonists believed they had to tame nature. They feared the wilderness and were convinced it was infested with wild beasts and savages. For centuries, settlers pressed across the continent, cutting down forests, damming rivers, constructing roads, laying rail lines, building cities, and industrializing the nation. For the most part, settlers did not question the wisdom of changing the environment to suit humans; it was called development and thought to be a sign of progress. That prompted Chief Seattle, leader of the Suquamish tribe in the Washington Territory, to warn in an 1855 letter, "Continue to contaminate your bed and one night you will suffocate in your own waste."[2]

The indigenous concept of protecting Mother Earth has been passed on over many generations. As an example, in 2009 teens from northern Michigan and Marquette, Michigan's Keweenaw Bay Indian Community, continued a program to protect bees and butterflies that pollinate and helped restore native plants to areas of the Upper Peninsula. Northern Cheyenne teens in Montana have renovated tribal homes to save energy. In the Northwest, Native American tribes have developed two large hydroelectric projects and a biomass project that operates on wood waste

It Happened to Nate and Danny

Sixteen-year-old Nate Pahe and twenty-three-year-old Danny Wyatt from the Washoe tribe of California and Nevada took part in the 2008 Longest Walk, which started on February 11 in San Francisco and ended in Washington, D.C., on July 11. The walk commemorated the 1978 Longest Walk to protest and lobby against proposed legislation before Congress that would have restricted tribal government, limited some hunting and fishing rights, and closed native schools and hospitals. According to a published report on the 2008 walk, "Both Wyatt and Pahe said the walk opened their eyes to issues including being respectful of native dead at historical sites, recognizing the effects of global warming and respecting the earth. 'The earth is being destroyed and we're not doing anything,' Pahe said. 'All native people have are their prayers.'" Walkers from more than one hundred Native American nations traveled by two different routes and carried prayers, often in the form of feathers attached to a sacred staff or pole. Pahe noted that his group walked about twenty miles each day: "There was something different every day and every day I was meeting new people. There were a lot of humble good people who walked each day." The walkers arrived in Washington, D.C., with the message "All life is sacred. Protect Mother Earth."[3]

from the lumber mill of the Confederated Tribes of Warm Springs in Oregon. The plant is expected to generate renewable electricity for more than 15,000 homes.

Early Conservation Efforts

Even though some Americans have exploited the nation's natural resources with devastating speed, many also have fought to protect the environment. In the late 1800s, three different kinds of environmental problems became matters of public debate. According to the National Park Service,

One problem was the prospect that the nation soon would run out of vital natural resources, especially wood. To ensure that future generations would have adequate supplies of essential raw materials, many people joined "the conservation movement." (That phrase first became popular in the first decade of the 20th century.) A second issue was the fate of "wilderness." A number of organizations began to argue that undeveloped lands of great natural beauty ought to be preserved. The third problem to attract attention before 1900 was pollution—a horrible threat to health in the nation's fast-growing cities. That threat led to far-reaching efforts to improve the urban environment.[4]

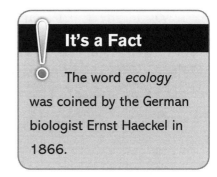

It's a Fact

The word *ecology* was coined by the German biologist Ernst Haeckel in 1866.

In spite of great opposition from industrialists, miners, ranchers, and others who believed natural resources should be available for commercial use whenever needed, conservationists convinced the U.S. Congress to pass legislation establishing national parks and forests and wilderness preserves. For example, in 1891 Congress passed the Forest Reserve Act, which empowered the president to create "forest reserves" and created the foundation for what became the National Forest System. Two years later, President Benjamin Harrison created thirteen million acres of forest reserves.

But with the Great Depression of the 1930s, funds to maintain these natural resources were not available. In 1933, during the early weeks of his presidency, Franklin D. Roosevelt proposed an emergency conservation measure to hire unmarried and unemployed young men between the ages of seventeen and twenty-eight to do forestry and flood-prevention work. Congress passed the act that established the Civilian Conservation Corps in April 1933. Four departments—labor, agriculture, interior, and the army—worked together to establish and operate the camps, which totaled 1,330 by the end of June 1933. The army ran the camps for the young men, who enlisted for six months and were paid thirty dollars per month. Paul Hughes, who was a Vermont teenager at the time, recalls:

I was in my third year of high school along with my friend, who eventually became my brother-in-law. We both decided we would try the CCC for the summer. It was probably one of the only opportunities for a high school kid to earn any money. And, in those days it was even hard to find a job bicycling for the Western Union, you know, it was. The work wasn't there for kids or for anybody else for that matter—work was tough.[5]

In a documentary about CCC veterans who were enlistees from Vermont, Lanyard Benoit remembers:

When I enlisted in the CCs, I was fifteen years old, and you should have been seventeen. But I was not the only young man in them CC camps. There were thousands and thousands of young kids that were fifteen, sixteen years old. They come off of farms—the poor people. . . . You got all your medication, your dental work, a good roof over your head, and ripping good meals every day.[6]

CCC veteran Roy Lemons went to a CCC camp at Grand Canyon, Arizona: "Here I was, seventeen, I'd quit school, I'd never had a job, a regular job, I would go to sleep at night hearing my brothers and sisters crying because they didn't have any food. I had lost all hope in the future, and suddenly there's this opportunity."[7]

By 1936, more then 500,000 young men had enrolled in the CCC. In 1937, the corps was extended for three more years. But after the United States entered World War II, the corps was abolished, and many enrollees joined the U.S. military. However, the corps' legacy is most apparent in national parks where the CCC built campgrounds, picnic areas, picnic tables, fireplaces, signs, exhibits, and other park structures and erected telephone poles and electric lights.

Tackling Pollution

After World War II, during the 1950s and 1960s, public attention focused on water and air pollution. Consider this: In the mid-1950s, a reported 155 tons of chemicals, metals, oil, and salts were dumped each day into the Cuyahoga River that runs through Cleveland, Ohio. The pollutants came from such industries as meat packers, oil refineries, steel plants, paint companies, and tar distilleries. Not only was the river foul smelling, but it also was highly flammable. Concentrations of methane gas and oil slicks caused the river surface to catch fire on several occasions. One spectacular blaze in 1969 burned over several miles through a murky industrial section of Cleveland. The fire finally convinced authorities at the local, state, and federal levels to clean up the Cuyahoga and other tributaries feeding into Lake Erie and other Great Lakes. Projects to clean up polluted rivers and streams across the United States and to prevent contamination of groundwater also got under way in the 1960s. Wetland preservation received attention as well. These efforts have continued into the second decade of the twenty-first century.

Besides tackling water pollution, the 1960s and 1970s were decades in which authorities and environmental groups in urban areas began to take action to curb air pollutants that were (and still are in some places) causing major health problems and killing trees and other plant life. A major air pollutant is smog. The term *smog* was coined in the early 1900s to refer to a combination of fog and black smoke that engulfed London, England, from coal-burning factories, businesses, and homes. In the United States, smog was first used in the 1940s to describe the air pollutants that cast a shroud over Los Angeles. But the smog that developed came from fog mixed with a variety of gaseous or chemical pollutants with the main component being gaseous ozone. The gas itself is not a pollutant and, in fact, is essential for life on earth. For example, in the stratosphere—the layer of air above the earth—ozone creates a shield that protects living things from ultraviolet rays of the sun. Without the protective layer of ozone, the well-being of every person on the planet is in jeopardy.

Smog ozone is another matter. When nitrogen oxides (NO_x) and volatile organic compounds (VOCs) combine with sunlight, they form ground-level ozone. The chemical compounds that lead to smog ozone come from motor vehicle emissions, manufacturing plants, and a variety of industries. When smog ozone occurs, it adversely affects the health of millions of Americans. If people already suffer such chronic diseases as asthma or heart disease, smog can aggravate their problems. Healthy individuals also may suffer lung dysfunction—coughing, "tightness" in the chest, or chest pain, for example—and such symptoms as burning eyes and sore throat. People involved in strenuous exercise are well advised to cut back when smog ozone levels are high.

Smog ozone also has an adverse effect on agriculture and forests. The yields of major cash crops like soybeans, corn, and wheat may be reduced, causing millions of dollars in losses to farmers. Trees and shrubs often die or are stunted in growth due to smog ozone. Because of its reactive nature, smog ozone also can damage manufactured goods and natural building materials. For example, it causes rubber to crack, dyes to fade, and paint to erode. Metal, concrete, and stone, particularly limestone, in various structures, such as bridges, monuments, and statues, may corrode.

High levels of smog trigger "smog alerts" in many U.S. cities, particularly in southern California. Serious efforts to control emissions from vehicles and industries that contribute to smog ozone began with the first Clean Air Act of 1963. The act provided funds for state and local agencies to establish regulations for air quality. But the regulations were not adequate, and by the end of the 1960s, it was clear that national standards were needed. The Clean Air Amendments of 1970 addressed that need. However, another twenty years later, tougher air pollution controls were required and resulted in the Clean Air Amendments of 1990. Currently, environmental groups are urging the Environmental Protection Agency (EPA) to enforce its new, more stringent regulations established in 2010. Those rules require that smog levels be lowered from seventy-five parts per billion to between sixty and seventy parts per billion, but they have been opposed by the petroleum industry and states that would have to implement the regulations at a high cost.[8]

When Mother Earth Got Her Day—And Then Some

It all began in the 1960s when U.S. senator Gaylord Nelson became concerned about the nation's polluted environment and persuaded President John F. Kennedy to conduct a tour highlighting the need for conservation and protecting the environment from degradation. Although Kennedy's tour did little to put environmental issues into the public consciousness, Nelson continued to speak publicly about the subject. In 1969 he held teach-ins on college campuses. At the time, teach-ins were demonstrations against the war in Vietnam, and Nelson got the idea to organize a huge grassroots protest over what was happening to the environment. As Nelson recalls:

> At a conference in Seattle in September 1969, I announced that in the spring of 1970 there would be a nationwide grassroots demonstration on behalf of the environment and invited everyone to participate. The wire services carried the story from coast to coast. The response was electric. It took off like gangbusters. Telegrams, letters, and telephone inquiries poured in from all across the country. The American people finally had a forum to express its concern about what was happening to the land, rivers, lakes, and air—and they did so with spectacular exuberance.[9]

Thus began the first Earth Day in 1970, with at least twenty million people involved across the United States. Ever since, Earth Day has been celebrated each year with one-day, weekend, or week-long festivities that include concerts, speeches, tree plantings, river and seashore cleanups, and numerous other activities. Worldwide more than a billion people every year now celebrate Earth Day.[10]

> **It's a Fact**
>
> During the year that the first Earth Day was celebrated, the Clean Air Act of 1970 passed. Two years later saw passage of the Water Pollution Control Act of 1972 and then the Endangered Species Act of 1973. Nevertheless, by the 1990s, other serious environmental hazards were making themselves known. Global warming and depletion of the ozone layer are a major concern, as is the possibility of another catastrophic event like the 2010 explosion at the BP Deepwater Horizon oil rig in the Gulf of Mexico that killed eleven workers and sent oil spewing into the gulf for three months.

In spite of all the celebrations and publicity about saving Mother Earth, some people believe that Earth Day is a political conspiracy, as two teenage girls in Calaveras County, California, discovered. Kati Giblin and Cierra Allen, Calaveras High School Earth Club members, appeared before the Calaveras County supervisors to ask them to designate April 15–22, 2011, as Earth Week. Their request "triggered an hour of debate on everything from climate change to economic sustainability," according to a news report. "We think sustainability is preserving the present quality of life," Giblin said. The chairman of the county supervisors disagreed and said that Earth Day was "part of a well-organized political agenda." Some in the audience declared that sustainability was part of a U.N. "effort to create a one-world government" or was a "socialist plot." One man, Peter Racz of the Gold Country Patriots, was convinced that climate change was a "fraud." He opined, "I feel sorry for the kids, because they are misled."[11] Yet others at the meeting supported the girls, and by a vote of three to two, the Earth Week designation became a fact for Calaveras County.

The naysayers in Calaveras County are not alone. TV commentators on Fox News declared after the BP oil spill that the disaster was a conspiracy by environmentalists and President Obama to destroy the petroleum industry, even though the oil companies have made huge profits and had hundreds of safety

See This Flick: *Hoot*

Based on the best-selling novel *Hoot* by Florida novelist  Carl Hiaasen, the movie by the same name (2006) tells the story of Roy, a young man who moves from Montana to Florida with his family. As the new kid, he soon becomes the target of a school bully, which doesn't surprise Roy because he has moved so often and being bullied is nothing new. The movie combines comedy and adventure as Roy becomes involved in a fight to protect a population of endangered owls. He's confronted by Beatrice, a tough girl whose brother is Mullet Fingers. The two are keeping watch on a flock of endangered burrowing owls that are threatened by a construction project that would destroy the owls' nest. Roy, Beatrice, and Mullet Fingers decide to take on crooked politicians and bumbling cops in the hope of saving their feathered friends. Who do you think wins?

---

violations. Rush Limbaugh, for example, implied on his show that the BP oil rig could have been blown up on purpose in order to stop more oil drilling.

Conservative bloggers also have charged that Earth Day is a "scam" and that warnings about climate change are not based on science. One blogger posited that Earth Day began and has continued as an ideological battle against industrialized society. Others charge that Earth Day is a pagan celebration. And still others are convinced that the day is somehow a communist conspiracy because the first celebration was held on the one-hundredth anniversary of the birth of Russian communist leader Vladimir Lenin (1870–1924), although subsequent Earth Days have marked the birth of such figures as naturalist John Muir (1838–1914), a strong advocate for wilderness protection.

Who Cares for the Earth?

Whatever the cynics and opponents of Earth Day have to say, individuals and communities across the United States participate in events to protect the planet.

In 2011, for example, teens conducted a cigarette litter cleanup at Tanglewood Park in Forsyth County, North Carolina. The event was sponsored by the TRU Youth Advisory Council, which used the slogan "The Earth Is Not an Ashtray" to call attention to the fact that cigarette litter has negative impacts on both human health and the environment.

At Veritas Classical School in Macon, Georgia, tree planting was on the agenda for Earth Day 2011. Macy Hall, a junior, said, "I love the outdoors. Any excuse to plant a tree is a good excuse to me."[12]

Miss USA Teen titleholders in various states had this to say about their activities for Earth Day 2011:

- Paige Higgerson of Illinois: "I plan to implement a 'Clean and Green' movement for the roads in my community. Living in rural Illinois, some of our roads are frequently overlooked in Adopt-a-Highway and other organized clean-up projects. I am banding together with citizens from my town to beautify our county roads by picking up trash and debris left by careless travelers."

- Audra Mari of North Dakota: "My community in Fargo . . . has curbside recycling that my family and neighbors actively participate in."

- Kayla Rousch of Oregon: "I will be planting a vegetable garden and recycling aluminum cans and plastic bottles on Earth Day."

- Morgan Smigel of Ohio: "To make our world more beautiful on Earth Day my school allows some of the students to spend the day outside, planting flowers and cleaning up the campus in lieu of class."

- Lindsey Bucci of Rhode Island: "To help save energy on Earth Day I will unplug all lamps and electronic devices when I'm not using them."

- Ana Rodriguez of Texas: "This year for Earth Day I will be visiting kids at the Children's Museum of Houston. I will be joining them in the 'Conservation Craze,' where we will all learn about ways to reduce, reuse and recycle."

- Bridget Martin of Vermont: "On Earth Day I am cleaning up our roads. Vermont is beautiful in the winter, but garbage tends to collect in snowbanks on the sides of roads, leaving a big clean-up job in the spring."

Cleaning up hazardous waste is one way to care for the earth.

Off the Bookshelf

The Green Book (2007), a *New York Times* bestseller by Elizabeth Rogers and Thomas M. Kostigen, is a helpful reference for anyone who is just beginning to investigate how to be a caretaker of the earth. The book contains lots of "simple steps" a person can take as well as brief overviews of green issues at stake. In addition, a dozen celebrities describe their green efforts. Also there are more than fifty pages of online references and their website addresses for further information.

- Ashley Golden of Wyoming: "Our schools in Gillette are very active when it comes to picking up trash and recycling. As a family, we recycle and help keep our neighborhood green and clean by picking up garbage whenever we see it."
- Elizabeth Heinen of Louisiana: "On Earth Day I am going to plant trees, pick up trash, conduct water quality tests and begin working on the first public nature trail in the area alongside students at the Wetland Watchers Celebration in Destrehan."
- Kay Tetreault of Massachusetts: "I will work to raise awareness at my high school by teaming up with our Environmental Club to encourage our peers to dispose of trash in separate recycling and composting bins. I'm also changing out all of the traditional lightbulbs in my house to compact fluorescent bulbs in order to conserve energy."
- Courtney Coleman of Hawaii: "This Earth Day I am encouraging Hawaiians to enjoy our stunning beaches and remember the importance of keeping them clean and litter free in an effort to protect our environment."

So it goes from east to west and north to south. Many more teen comments are available on the Miss Universe website.[13]

It Happened to the San Francisco Peaks

For years, Native Americans have protested the desecration of a religious site—a mountain range near Flagstaff, Arizona, known as the San Francisco Peaks, the highest range. There had been a small ski resort there since the 1930s, but with the permission of the U.S. Forest Service, a full-scale Snowball Resort that included lodges and restaurants was constructed in the 1970s. On the eastern slopes of the mountain, a pumice mine operated but was ordered closed in 1999 because of violations of the federal Clean Water Act. Meantime, though, the ski resort remains open, and thirteen tribes, including the Hopi and Navajo, have objected strongly. The Peaks are sacred Indian lands—home to spiritual entities. Alberta Nells, a 2009 teenage youth leader of the Navajo Nation, has been an outspoken opponent, explaining that the Peaks range is

one of our sacred mountains, and that those sacred mountains to us we call as our grandmother and as our Mother. . . . that mountain that we're protecting represents a woman. We call the water a woman, which is Mother Earth, we call it a female mountain. And we don't think of it as just as another mountain but as a family member—we respect it in the same way we would respect an elder or a grandmother. And we honor in that way, so that in a way you could kind of say I am a female helping another female, because that's what it represents; it represents our mother that provides us with the herbs and the medicines for our ceremony. And with that mountain there are the plants up there as well.[14]

Native Americans visit the mountain, valleys, lakes, and caves for religious ceremonies or to collect medicinal plants. They do not want this natural resource and holy place defiled. However, in 2004, the Forest Service permitted the ski resort to use treated sewage water to make artificial snow to spread on the slopes, which Native Americans considered a particularly offensive desecration. In addition, there are health concerns regarding the sewage water. Tribes continue their protests and demands that natural native religious sites be strictly protected.

Riding High for the Environment

High school students in the South Bronx have organized a program called EcoRyders. Older students teach middle school students about the urban environment by helping community gardeners and discussing environmental issues. As an incentive to participate in this program, students create skateboards. They order parts, paint boards, attach the trucks, and learn skateboarding tricks.

Although it is clear that many earth-saving events take place at least one day each year, a major challenge is finding ways to live green every day. To help in that regard, thousands of volunteers worldwide work to conserve and protect the earth's natural resources. They may take part in missions to save rain forests or to preserve seacoasts or offshore ocean waters from oil drilling. Although many environmental projects are global or national in scope, people working in their own backyards or communities carry out some of the most effective caretaking efforts. People from all walks of life are learning that they can do something to reduce or eliminate use of materials that pollute, and conserve nonrenewable resources. That includes an important component: reducing the amount of chemical substances that contribute to global warming.

Notes

1. Sharlene Irete, "All Life Is Sacred: Protect Mother Earth," *Vermonters Concerned on Native American Affairs*, October 17, 2008, http://vcnaa.com/native/content/view/555/2 (accessed May 3, 2011).
2. Chief Seattle, "Message to the Modern World," *Studies in Comparative Religion*, Summer 1976, www.studiesincomparativereligion.com/public/articles/Message_to_the_Modern_World-by_Chief_Seattle.aspx (accessed May 29, 2011).
3. Sharlene Irete, "All Life Is Sacred: Protect Mother Earth," *Vermonters Concerned on Native American Affairs*, October 17, 2008, http://vcnaa.com/native/content/view/555/2 (accessed May 3, 2011).
4. National Park Service, *History in the National Park Service*, n.d., www.nps.gov/history/history/hisnps/NPSThinking/nps-oah.htm (accessed May 3, 2011).

5. Steve Delaney and Lynne McCrea, *Those CCC Boys*, documentary, *Vermont Public Radio*, August 19, 2008, www.vpr.net/episode/43879 (accessed May 3, 2011).

6. Delaney and McCrea, *Those CCC Boys*, documentary.

7. Delaney and McCrea, *Those CCC Boys*, documentary.

8. Gavin Aronsen, "When Will Obama's EPA Crack Down on Smog?" *Mother Jones*, June 8, 2011, http://motherjones.com/blue-marble/2011/06/when-will-epa-crack-down-dangerous-smog (accessed June 27, 2011).

9. Gaylord Nelson, "How the First Earth Day Came About," n.d., http://earthday.envirolink.org/history.html (accessed May 6, 2011).

10. Earth Day Network, www.earthday.org/about-us (accessed May 7, 2011).

11. Union Democrat Staff, "Two Supes Over-React at Calaveras County Board Meeting," *The Union Democrat*, April 19, 2011, www.uniondemocrat.com/20110419103316/Opinion/Editorials/Two-Supes-over-react-at-Calaveras-County-Board-meeting (accessed November 8, 2011).

12. Haley Ricks, "Macon Teens Go Green to Mark Earth Day," April 19, 2011, www.macon.com/2011/04/19/1530271/teens-go-green-to-mark-earth-day.html (accessed May 7, 2011).

13. Miss Universe Organization, www.missuniverse.com/earth-day (accessed May 9, 2011).

14. Marianne Schnall, "Conversation with Alberta Nells," *feminist.com*, September 13, 2009, www.feminist.com/resources/artspeech/interviews/albertanells.html (accessed August 12, 2011).

LEAVING A LOW CARBON FOOTPRINT

"We want action . . . now because we want a livable future."
—Mia Szarvas, a high school senior and president of her school's Sustainability Club[1]

"Operation Bus Stop": That was the name of the project that three teenagers in Redding, Connecticut, undertook in 2009. Caitlin Taylor, Patrick Murphy, and Fallon Murphy developed a plan to reorganize school bus routes in order to reduce carbon emissions—or carbon footprints. At the time, the three teens noticed that some buses had many empty seats. As Patrick notes, "The way the bus service is being used is wasteful and harmful to the environment." The teenagers plotted bus routes and "determined that they could eliminate one route, which would save an estimated 4,440 to 5,550 pounds of carbon emissions a month," according to an online report. The trio submitted their plan to school officials, who promised to consider it. Patrick explains, "I realized by taking part in this project how just sheer organization can help save our environment. I am looking forward to continuing this pursuit and hopefully convincing our community that it is worth the time and effort it takes to make sure we are not wasteful."[2]

The Redding team through its "Operation Bus Stop" obviously developed a plan for leaving a low carbon footprint. But what is a carbon footprint? It is a "measure of the impact our activities have on the environment, and in particular climate change. It relates to the amount of greenhouse gases produced in our day-to-day lives." Greenhouse gases in the atmosphere include carbon dioxide (CO_2) and trace gases, such as water vapor, methane, and ozone. Thus, as the website explains,

The carbon footprint is a measurement of all greenhouse gases we individually produce and has units of tonnes (or kg) of carbon dioxide equivalent. A carbon footprint is made up of the sum of two parts, the primary footprint and the secondary footprint.

The **primary footprint** is a measure of our direct emissions of CO_2 from the burning of fossil fuels including domestic energy consumption and transportation (e.g., car and plane). We have direct control of these. The **secondary footprint** is a measure of the indirect CO_2 emissions from the whole lifecycle of products we use—those associated with their manufacture and eventual breakdown. To put it very simply—the more we buy, the more emissions will be caused on our behalf.[3]

Increase in Greenhouse Gases

The supply of CO_2 and other trace gases has been fairly stable for millions of years, helping to maintain a delicate balance between the solar energy reaching earth and the heat radiating out. Billions of tons of atmospheric CO_2 are removed from the atmosphere by oceans and growing plants, also known as "sinks," or natural pools and reservoirs. In a process known as photosynthesis, plants capture sunlight and use solar energy to combine CO_2 and water, producing glucose, an important source of energy for people and animals. During photosynthesis, plants give off oxygen as a waste product; this is inhaled by animals and people, who in turn exhale the carbon dioxide produced when food is oxidized, or used by their bodies. Thus, living plants and animals are one source of CO_2 released into the atmosphere. When in balance, the total carbon dioxide emissions and removals from the entire carbon cycle are roughly equal.

However, since the Industrial Revolution began centuries ago, human activities, particularly fossil-fuel combustion, have increased CO_2 concentrations in the atmosphere. Fossil fuels include coal, natural gas, and oil, and when they are burned, carbon dioxide is released. Because trees hold CO_2, the destruction of forests also contributes significantly to the increase in greenhouse gases. In 2005, global atmospheric concentrations of CO_2 were 35 percent higher than they were before the Industrial Revolution, according to the Environmental Protection Agency (EPA). Those high concentrations of carbon dioxide cause an enhanced greenhouse effect and what is known as *global warming*.

Along with CO_2, greenhouse gases include nitrous oxide (N_2O), which is emitted during agricultural and industrial activities as well as during incineration of fossil fuels and solid waste. Methane (CH_4), another greenhouse gas, comes from the production and transport of coal, natural gas, and oil; from livestock and other agricultural practices; and by the decay of organic waste in municipal solid waste landfills. According to the EPA, hydrofluorocarbons (HFCs) are "synthetic, powerful greenhouse gases that are emitted from a variety of industrial processes. . . . These gases are typically emitted in smaller quantities, but because they are potent greenhouse gases, they are sometimes referred to as High Global Warming Potential gases." The EPA predicts, "Many, but not all, human sources of greenhouse gas emissions are expected to rise in the future. This growth may be reduced by ongoing efforts to increase the use of newer, cleaner technologies and other measures. Additionally, our everyday choices about such things as commuting, housing, electricity use, and recycling can influence the amount of greenhouse gases being emitted."[4] That in turn can help reduce global warming or climate change.

The Climate Change Controversy

More than a century ago, scientists were linking climate change to the composition of chemicals in the atmosphere. In 1896, a Swedish chemist referred to the phenomenon as the *greenhouse effect*, thus coining a term. He noted similarities between the earth's atmosphere and the glass enclosures of a greenhouse: Both allow the sunlight to enter but prevent most of the solar heat from escaping. The greenhouse effect on earth is a natural condition. Sunlight that reaches the earth passes through a blanket of atmospheric gasses. The sun's energy is absorbed by land, water, and living organisms, but some of the energy goes back into space. Without greenhouse gases, too much heat would escape, and the earth would probably be too cold to sustain life. But because the carbon dioxide content of the earth's atmosphere has been increasing at a rapid rate, an enhanced greenhouse effect has been created, causing global warming, or climate change.

Numerous scientific studies have confirmed that global warming is taking place. In 2007, the Intergovernmental Panel on Climate Change (IPCC) of the United Nations, which includes scientists and technicians from around the world, issued one of its periodic reports stating, "Warming of the climate system is unequivocal, as is now evident from observations of increases in global average air and ocean temperatures, widespread melting of snow and ice and rising global average sea level."[5] Nevertheless, skeptics continue to argue that "Global Warming Talk Is All Just Hot Air" (newsmax.com) or that "Global Warming Is Bunk" (Fox News).

Some of their comments have been widely publicized. For example, U.S. senator James Inhofe of Oklahoma often has ridiculed those who warn about global warming. He once noted that "advocates of alarmism have grown increasingly desperate to try to convince the public that global warming is the greatest moral issue of our generation."[6] Another skeptic is S. Fred Singer, a physicist at George Mason University, who said in a PBS interview, "Climate change is a natural phenomenon. Climate keeps changing all the time. The fact that climate changes is not in itself a threat, because, obviously, in the past human beings have adapted to all kinds of climate changes."[7] One more major doubter is Richard Lindzen, an astrophysicist at the Massachusetts Institute of Technology. He is an outspoken critic of the many scientists who say that human activities contribute to global warming and accuses those scientists of intimidating dissenters and spreading "junk science."[8]

In 2006, former vice president Al Gore released his book and award-winning documentary *An Inconvenient Truth*, which was shown hundreds of times across the United States and in other countries. The documentary is an urgent call for action to reduce global warming and climate change. Although the film has raised awareness of climate change, it also has been criticized strongly by climate change skeptics. Critics charged that the film is alarmist and that there are inaccuracies and exaggerations in statements. "Michael Oppenheimer, a professor of geosciences and international affairs at Princeton who advised Mr. Gore on the book and movie" agreed with some arguments the critics made, according to the *New York Times*. But Oppenheimer notes, "On balance, he [Gore] did quite well—a credible and entertaining job on a difficult subject. . . . For that, he deserves a lot of credit. If you rake him over the coals, you're going to find people who disagree. But in terms of the big picture, he got it right."[9]

In May 2011, four hundred scientists held a conference in Denmark to discuss the rise in Arctic temperature, which is melting glaciers faster than expected. The scientists concluded that, because of the melts, sea levels will rise nearly three feet and perhaps up to five feet by 2100. As levels rise, Florida's long coastline, for one, that will be affected. In fact, it already has seen changes, with a pine forest that is now a tidal marsh because of rising sea levels. But Florida Republican governor Rick Scott, who took office in 2011, has said repeatedly that he does not believe that climate change is due to human activities. And most of the Florida legislature agrees.

However, in New York City, Mayor Michael Bloomberg has an entirely different view. He knows that the city not only contributes to greenhouse gas emissions but also could be affected by climate change—for example flooding from rising sea levels. According to a report, *Rolling Carbon: Greenhouse Gas Emissions from Commuting in New York City*, the mayor has called for:

a 30 percent cut in citywide greenhouse gas emissions from [2008] levels by 2030. Mayor Bloomberg's plan calls for emissions reductions across all sectors: buildings, power generation, and transportation. For most New Yorkers, commuting is a scheduled, routine activity performed twice a

Weather versus Climate

The EPA has *A Student's Guide to Global Climate Change* online. The website has varied sections, with one specifically explaining the difference between weather and climate:

> *Weather* is a specific event or condition that happens over a period of hours or days. For example, a thunderstorm, a snowstorm, and today's temperature all describe the weather.
>
> *Climate* refers to the average weather conditions in a place over many years (usually at least 30 years). For example, the climate in Minneapolis is cold and snowy in the winter, while Miami's climate is hot and humid. The average climate around the world is called global climate. Weather conditions can change from one year to the next. For example, Minneapolis might have a warm winter one year and a much colder winter the next. This kind of change is normal. But when the average pattern over many years changes, it could be a sign of climate change.
>
> Here's an easy way to remember the difference between weather and climate: Climate helps you decide what clothes to buy, and weather helps you decide what clothes to wear each day.[10]

day, 250 times per year. Because of this repetitiveness, the environmental impacts of one single commute are multiplied 500 times over throughout the year. On average, each commuter in New York City causes the emission of about 3.5 pounds of carbon dioxide per one-way commute for a total of 1,750 pounds of CO_2 each year. However, actual commuting emissions can be much higher or lower, depending on distance and, especially, mode choice: an average commute by passenger vehicle causes the emission of over 4,000 pounds of CO_2 per year, while another of the same distance via

What Teens Know about Climate Change

A Yale University survey of 517 teenagers in April 2011 found that 57 percent of them say that global warming is caused mostly by human activities; 77 percent of teens understand that the greenhouse effect refers to gases in the atmosphere that trap heat; 52 percent of teens understand that carbon dioxide traps heat from the earth's surface; and 71 percent of teens know that carbon dioxide is produced by the burning of fossil fuels.[11]

subway is responsible for just 820 pounds of CO_2. A walking or bicycling commute generates zero CO_2 emissions.

On a citywide scale, combined CO_2 emissions from these individual commutes form a significant portion of New York City's total greenhouse gas emissions. Every year, approximately 3.5 million New Yorkers commute a total distance of over 11.5 billion miles.[12]

"We Want Action"

In spite of global warming skeptics, the Students for Sustainability Club at Analy High School in Sebastopol, California, organized a march in May 2011 to promote action on climate change. High school senior, lead organizer, and president of the club Mia Szarvas told a reporter, "We want action . . . now because we want a livable future."[13]

Two Cottonwood High School teens in Utah, Abrianna Peto and Max McLeod, also are taking action. They belong to a Polar Bear Club, which is part of an international effort to protect polar bears who are being threatened by the global warming that has diminished summer sea ice in the Arctic; the bears need the ice to move from place to place to hunt for seals, their main food source. Peto and McLeod entered a competition sponsored by Polar Bears International to find ways to lower their community's carbon footprint and reduce the melting of polar ice caps. They reduced the use of nonbiodegradable Styrofoam and took other green initiatives. According to a news report, "The students estimate their efforts have reduced more than 21,000 pounds of carbon dioxide emissions."[14]

In Louisville, Kentucky, high school seniors Emily Goldstein and Brandie Farkas also took up the polar bear cause. With the support of the Louisville Zoo, they entered the Project Polar Bear contest, creating a website (www.louisvillezoo .org/projectpolarbear) dedicated to stopping climate change. Goldstein says, "With this website, we want to share with everyone that it is up to us all to halt global climate change, and every single person can make a difference. . . . If everyone would make even small changes in their lifestyles, it would add up to make the big changes necessary to save not only the polar bears, but the whole planet."[15]

In Pittsburgh, Pennsylvania, student teams from three school districts also participated in the competition. One team called Bearnecessities raised money to plant 1,500 trees. Another team called Make It Happen gathered pledges from students and community members to cut their energy use. Energy Angels, a third team, distributed compact fluorescent light bulbs. One team member explains, "A lot of people wondered what compact fluorescent bulbs had to do with polar bears and we had to explain that by changing to a compact fluorescent bulb you are saving energy, reducing your carbon footprint and reducing global warming, which is reducing the ice cap that the polar bears float on." The team estimates that "over the lifetime of the 1,958 bulbs distributed, they will decrease carbon dioxide emissions by 1.55 million pounds."[16]

To learn about the effects of global warming, twenty high school students from various states attended a month-long workshop in 2009 at the North Cascades National Park in Washington State. The workshop was designed to show students how warming trends are melting glaciers and affecting ecosystems in the park. Students hiked up steep mountainsides, waded into streams, and observed the wilderness area. Scientists and park officials hoped the students would be

Polar bears like this one are endangered because of global warming.

conservation and/or recycling activists in their own communities. Teenager Donya Borham of Washington, D.C., notes that her family was not particularly aware of climate change: "When I was at home, I used to always encourage them to turn off the lights . . . because I didn't want the bill to be high. Now that I know more about climate change, that's a bigger reason." Another teenager, Heather McPherson from Shoreline, Washington, explains, "A lot of times, you get discouraged, wondering what impact you can make." But for her the workshop was an inspiring experience: "It's really great to see there are so many people rooting for you."[17]

Global warming is also a concern for members of an Alaska high school group called Alaska Youth for Environmental Action (AYEA), which is part of the National Wildlife Federation. According to a 2008 news report, "The club has been recognized locally and statewide and also received a national award for its work on education about global warming and environmental efforts." Anna Rix, an Anchorage senior, says that "AYEA has increased my knowledge and awareness

Eco-friendly lightbulbs can help reduce carbon footprints.

> ## Paper versus Foam Containers
>
> For years those polystyrene foam containers—from beverage cups to carryout boxes—were considered harmful for the environment. Paper containers were thought to be more eco-friendly than those made of foam. But a peer-reviewed study released in 2011 finds that manufacturing polystyrene foam cups, plates, and sandwich containers takes significantly less energy and water than manufacturing comparable paper-based or corn-based (polylactic, or PLA) alternatives. A single-coated paperboard cup with a sleeve produces almost twice the amount of greenhouse gases, which contribute to global warming, than one polystyrene foam cup.[18]

of environmental issues as we have seen presentations on electronics recycling and global warming." Members of AYEA share what they have learned with their community and often make presentations about the environment at elementary schools. As senior Wiley Carson explains, "When we distribute compact fluorescent bulbs or recycle cans, it is not just about how much carbon that one bulb will save or conserving the one can, it is about starting to act locally—even in your own home—and seeing that action spread around the state, the country and even the globe."[19]

Calculating and Reducing Carbon Footprints

Numerous websites offer interactive calculators to determine the carbon footprint for an individual, family, business, school, community, state, or even the entire nation. If you access a carbon calculator, it will usually require you to answer a variety of questions, and your responses determine how much you contribute to global warming. For example, the Nature Conservancy has a calculator that asks about home energy use, driving and flying, food and diet, and recycling and waste.[20] The EPA has a calculator that provides an estimate of your personal or family's

From the Bookshelf

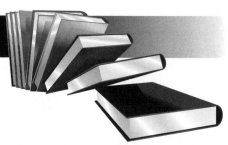

The Green Teen Book: The Eco-Friendly Teen's Guide to Saving the Planet (2009) by Jenn Savedge is a handy-sized paperback that has many practical suggestions for living green. One chapter, for example, tells how to save energy and reduce carbon footprints. The chapter includes an interview with Avery Hairston, who at age fifteen with ten friends launched Relight NY (relightny .com). In answering a question about what inspired him, Hairston responds, "I saw this slide show by Al Gore (this was before *An Inconvenient Truth*) that alerted me to the problem of global warming. Then one day I was reading the *New York Times* and I came across a full-page ad taken out by Starbucks that said that if every reader of the *New York Times* switched just one lightbulb to a CFL [compact fluorescent lightbulb], it would be like taking 89,000 cars off the road because CFLs save so much energy. . . . I thought it would be great for young people to tackle that." Through Relight NY Hairston and his friends raised money to buy CFLs and distribute them to low-income families and at the same time "spread the word about global warming."[23]

---

greenhouse gas emissions and explores the impact of taking various actions to reduce your emissions.[21] On some website calculators, you may be asked about the meals you eat, car you drive (or don't drive), how much you use the computer, how often you turn off lights and electrical equipment, and other choices that you make. Then your carbon footprint is displayed.

Reducing one's carbon footprint is another matter. What if you can't afford a hybrid car that is supposed to be more eco-friendly than a gasoline-powered car? Perhaps solar panels, which save energy, are too expensive for your family to install. However, there are other smaller but effective steps to take. Consider bottled water, which has a major carbon footprint because it comes in small plastic bottles that are shipped long distances. Americans consume thirty billion single-serve bottles of

The Green Youth Movement (GYM)

Reducing global warming is a major part of the GYM, founded by teenager Ally Maize of Los Angeles, California, when she was a high school freshman in 2007. At the time, she was preparing for her learner's driving permit, and she was concerned about the type of vehicle her parents would buy once she had her driver's license. As she puts it,

I had been studying about the detrimental state of our environment in school and started reading more and more about the pressing issue of global warming. I explained to my mom and dad that when we did get that new car, it had to be a hybrid. I wanted to start making a difference in our family and it was very important to me. I started to do more research on the web about different hybrids, and concurrently, I started learning more about the global warming issue.

As Ally shared what she had learned with her family, changes were made in her household: "We changed our hot water heating system inside our house to tank-less, and added solar panels on our roof. We started using only reusable grocery bags and stopped using the plastic. Together we came up with the idea to start GYM, an organization started by a youth to educate people about global warming and pressing environmental issues."[24] The nonprofit GYM initiates numerous events to inform kids and teens about living green and taking small steps to help ensure a sustainable future.

In 2010, the editors of *Green Living* interviewed Ally and asked about her future goals for GYM. She says,

I hope to one day garner the support of politicians and educators to create a practical and research based environmental course of study that would ultimately become integrated in every elementary school education curriculum across the nation. It is my belief that providing youth with meaningful and practical methods of conserving and utilizing resources is the key to changing the direction of global warming. As the effects of global warming continue to advance from a theoretical construct to a reality, it is necessary that each of us assume responsibility to make a difference. Establishing the Green Youth Movement has been my way to embrace what I regard as one of the most significant issues that plagues our future.[25]

water each year, which means that producing that many plastic bottles puts more than 2.5 million tons of carbon dioxide into the earth's upper atmosphere annually. To reduce your carbon footprint, you can carry water in a reusable bottle or canteen. Also, you can reduce the time your television is on. Watch the television 2.5 hours less each day and cut CO_2 by 100 pounds per year. An hour less with the computer and monitor turned on saves 37.7 pounds of CO_2 per year.

In spring 2009, ten teens in St. Louis, Missouri, spent their Saturday nights studying the effects of climate change on amphibians—frogs, toads, and salamanders—which are diminishing in number and may suffer more losses due to global warming. The project was conducted by the St. Louis Science Center and is part of the National Science Foundation's effort to get everyday citizens involved in monitoring signs of climate change in their communities. The St. Louis teenagers put on boots and headlamps, carried recorders, tested water, and made observations of amphibians at a local pond. Their findings were submitted to a "nationwide citizen science website called Frogwatch USA which compiles data submitted from all over so that scientists can use it in their research."[22]

Notes

1. Brett Wilkison, "Sebastopol Teens Organize March to Highlight Climate Change," *The Press Democrat*, May 8, 2011, www.pressdemocrat.com/article/20110508/ARTICLES/110509522 (accessed May 10, 2011).

2. Joan Lownds, "Bus Route Project Picks Up Prize for 'Green' Teens," *The ReddingPilot.com*, March 20, 2009, www.acorn-online.com/joomla15/index.php?option=com_content&view =article&id=22884:bus-route-project-picks-up-prize-for-green-teens&catid=43:redding- around-town&Itemid=1170 (accessed May 9, 2011).

3. "What Is a Carbon Footprint?" *Carbon Footprint*, 2011, www.carbonfootprint.com/carbon- footprint.html (accessed May 10, 2011).

4. "Greenhouse Gas Emissions," *U.S. Environmental Protection Agency*, April 20, 2011, http:// epa.gov/climatechange/emissions/index.html (accessed May 15, 2011).

5. Intergovernmental Panel on Climate Change, *Climate Change 2007: Synthesis Report Summary for Policymakers*, www.ipcc.ch/pdf/assessment-report/ar4/syr/ar4_syr_spm.pdf (accessed May 10, 2011).

6. "Climate Variance No Crisis, Says Senate Committee Chair," *The Heartland Institute*, De- cember 2006, www.heartland.org/publications/environment%20climate/article/20253/Cli- mate_Variance_No_Crisis_Says_Senate_Committee_Chair.html (accessed May 10, 2011).

7. S. Fred Singer interview with Jon Palfreman, "What's Up with the Weather?" *Frontline/Nova*, 2000, www.pbs.org/wgbh/warming/debate/singer.html (accessed May 10, 2011).

8. Richard Lindzen, "Climate of Fear: Global-Warming Alarmists Intimidate Dissenting Scien- tists into Silence," *Wall Street Journal*, April 12, 2006.

9. William J. Broad, "From a Rapt Audience, A Call to Cool the Hype," *New York Times*, March 13, 2007, www.nytimes.com/2007/03/13/science/13gore.html (accessed May 15, 2011).

10. U.S. Environmental Protection Agency, "Weather versus Climate," *A Student's Guide to Global Climate Change*, April 13, 2011, www.epa.gov/climatechange/kids/basics/concepts.html (ac- cessed May 13, 2011).

11. Anthony Leiserowitz, Nicholas Smith, and Jennifer R. Marlon, "American Teens' Knowl- edge of Climate Change," *Yale Project on Climate Change Communication*, April 18, 2011, http://environment.yale.edu/climate/files/American_Teens_Knowledge_of_Climate_Change American%20Teens%20Knowledge%20of%20Climate%20Change (accessed May 10, 2011).

12. Transalt.org, *Rolling Carbon: Greenhouse Gas Emissions from Commuting in New York City*, Oc- tober 2008, www.transalt.org/files/newsroom/reports/rolling_carbon.pdf (accessed May 15, 2011).

13. Brett Wilkison, "Sebastopol Teens Organize March to Highlight Climate Change," *The Press Democrat*, May 8, 2011, www.pressdemocrat.com/article/20110508/ARTICLES/110509522 (accessed May 10, 2011).

14. "2 Utah Teens Are Helping Save Polar Bears," *Deseret News*, March 14, 2009, www.deseret- news.com/article/1,5143,705290952,00.html (accessed May 11, 2011).

15. Kara Bussabarger, "Louisville Zoo Volunteers Emily Goldstein and Brandie Farkas Win Proj- ect Polar Bear," *zandavisitor.com*, May 4, 2009, www.zandavisitor.com/newsarticle-1377- Louisville_Zoo_Volunteers_Emily_Goldstein_and_Brandie_Farkas_Win_Project_Polar_Bear (accessed July 3, 2011).

16. Mary Niederberger, "Local Teens Compete to Stop the Meltdown," *Pittsburgh Post-Gazette*, January 13, 2011, www.post-gazette.com/pg/11013/1117421-54.stm (accessed May 15, 2011).

17. Associated Press, "Local Students Hike to Learn about Climate Change," *KOMO News*, August 2, 2009, www.komonews.com/news/local/52308292.html (accessed May 13, 2011).

18. Franklin Associates, "Life Cycle Inventory of Foam Polystyrene, Paper-Based, and PLA Foodservice Products," February 4, 2011, http://plasticfoodservicefacts.com/Life-Cycle-Inventory-Foodservice-Products (accessed May 12, 2011). See also William Rathje and Cullen Murphy, "Five Major Myths about Garbage, and Why They're Wrong," *Smithsonian*, July 1992.

19. Stacey Wheeler, "Thinking Green: Teen Group Works to Educate Public on Environment," *Tuscaloosanews.com*, April 29, 2008, www.tuscaloosanews.com/article/20080429/PULSE02/914932084?Title=Thinking-green-Teen-group-works-to-educate-public-on-environment (accessed May 14, 2011).

20. See www.nature.org/greenliving/carboncalculator (accessed May 14, 2011).

21. See www.epa.gov/climatechange/emissions/ind_calculator.html (accessed May 14, 2011).

22. Joyce Gramza, "Teens, Frogs, and Climate Change," *Science Central*, May 21, 2009, www.sciencentral.com/video/2009/05/21/teens-frogs (accessed October 22, 2011). See also "Wildlife Watch," *National Wildlife Federation*, 2011, www.nwf.org/WildlifeWatch (accessed May 16, 2011).

23. Jenn Savedge, *The Green Teen Book: The Eco-Friendly Teen's Guide to Saving the Planet* (Gabriola Island, BC: New Society, 2009), pp. 85–86.

24. Ally Maize, "Ally's Story," *greenyouthmovement.org*, 2009, http://greenyouthmovement.org/About-GYM/My-Story.html (accessed August 5, 2011).

25. "The Green Profile: Ally Maize," *greenlivingonline.com*, May 18, 2010, www.greenlivingonline.com/article/green-profile-ally-maize (accessed August 5, 2011).

USING LESS FOSSIL FUEL

"I've tried to involve myself as much as I could with environmental causes,
culminating with my founding of Students for Solar Schools."
—teenager Adam Roudonis of California[1]

In cartoons the lightbulb goes on over someone's head. It's a common way to depict "Now, there's an idea!" or an aha! moment or "I just got it!" But those incandescent lightbulbs may seem out of place for people living green because they have changed to compact fluorescent bulbs or light-emitting diodes (LED) bulbs, as many teenagers have discovered during their efforts to reduce energy and carbon footprints.

Along with efforts to change lightbulb use, some teens are urging their peers and others to use Blackle as a search engine on the Web. Blackle is similar to Google, but unlike Google with a white screen, Blackle has a predominantly black screen and requires less power than a bright white screen. They also urge others to use natural light whenever possible, switch off electric lights when leaving a room, turn off computers, and unplug cell phone chargers and small appliances like coffeemakers and toasters, all of which pull electricity even when not in use. Other teens are making efforts to convince their families to set their home thermostats a few degrees lower in the winter and a few degrees higher in the summer and use fans to save energy and utility costs.

Two teenage girls, Daniela Lapidous and Shreya Indukuri at Harker School in San Jose, California, began a project in 2009 to reduce energy use not only in their school but also in other schools in California. Lapidous and Indukuri initiated

A Blog from an Environmental Protection Agency (EPA) Intern

Ameshia Cross is an intern in EPA's Air and Radiation Division in Chicago. She wrote the message below in April 2011, posting it on Greenversations, EPA's official blog:

As a teen when I heard the word energy I automatically thought of coffee, sugary snacks, and anything that could get me through the day. Unfortunately that is not where energy that powers our daily lives—home, school, work, etc.—comes from! During my time serving as president of my high school's Green Club, one of my tasks was developing ideas for alternative energy sources and teaching middle and elementary school kids about the importance of energy conservation. Today kids have taken energy conservation to the next level and their efforts are truly inspiring.

The Minnesota Student Energy Project (MNSEP) is a student-founded, student-led non-profit that began in 2008. What started as three high school students with an idea to raise money for solar panels for their school, Mayo High School, has expanded to include numerous students across the state. What the teens didn't expect was the amount of money and interest that their project would spark. Local media became interested. Other schools and community leaders wanted to talk with the students about how they developed such a strong resource base and what they could do to help expand MNSEP's efforts.

[In 2011] MNSEP caught the eyes and ears of Minnesota legislators, national news, and regional organizations. The young people that make up MNSEP are on the move making sustainable change. Through grants from the Federal Department of Energy and numerous other organizations, MNSEP is spreading its goal of educating communities on alternative energy and conservation.

We can all learn something from the MNSEP members about energy and unity. They took a small group and turned it into something bigger because they had a goal and a dream to see a sustainable future for generations to come. From the looks of things, they are going to keep dreaming and achieving.[2]

a website, SmartPowerEd.org, designed for teenagers who want to help their schools save energy. The website explains that they "primarily endorse the use of smart sub-meter devices with a public dashboard

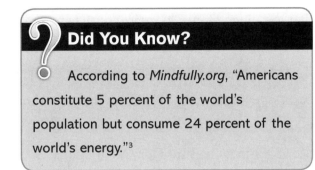

Did You Know?

According to *Mindfully.org*, "Americans constitute 5 percent of the world's population but consume 24 percent of the world's energy."[3]

software for schools to understand and reduce their energy use without major facility overhauls." The software provides an at-a-glance view of energy use and provides a "school access to a live data feed of energy use per building, at any hour of the day, in various units. In contrast, normal meters only measure total use over a set period of time and do not allow as thorough of an understanding."[4]

Indukuri explains that the "great thing about the program is that it requires students' involvement and interest in energy reduction which ultimately lowers the school's carbon footprint. Most schools are very enthusiastic about having a smart energy solution because the energy they conserve means saving money for the school—money that can be used for other projects." Lapidous declares, "One of our goals is to get smart energy moving in at least 25 schools in California." Another Harker student, Olivia Zhu, has written about the girls' work and presented it at the 2009 Climate Change Conference in Copenhagen, Denmark, where it got "rave reviews."[5]

Energy Patrols

Helping others conserve energy is what energy patrols in schools are all about. Across the United States, students take part in a program to patrol the schools to monitor energy use. The patrols have such varied names as Wattchdog, Wattwatchers, and Watt Busters, and they use a variety of methods to determine how much energy is used in their schools and what can be done about reducing it. In the New York City area, a Friends (Quaker) school uses Kill-A-Watt meters that are plugged into electrical outlets where devices like computers are plugged in. The Kill-A-Watt meters assess how much energy is wasted.

In Cupertino, California, a school was able to save about one third of its energy costs—approximately $1,000 per month—through its energy patrol. In Cincinnati, Ohio, five teenagers were part of a Green Team that got jobs monitoring energy use at National Institute for Occupational Safety and Health (NIOSH) facilities in the city. They conducted an inventory of personal appliances being used by the six hundred or so employees at three sites. The inventory, NIOSH says, could help convince employees to cut their energy use.

Watt Busters at Douglass High School in Memphis, Tennessee, hand out tickets to those in the school who waste energy. To save energy, they also unplug computers and turn off lights when not needed. From September 1, 2009, to October 21, 2010, the school saved $14,906 in energy costs and diminished its carbon footprint by 234,708 pounds of CO_2 emissions.[6]

In Pasco County, Florida, students who monitor for conservation call themselves "Earth Patrols," and like energy patrols elsewhere, they make the rounds in their schools to check for lights left on, recyclables in trash cans, leaky faucets, and litter. At elementary schools students wear green vests to identify themselves as patrols, and at high schools students wear lanyards with their identification cards. If patrols find classrooms and areas where conservation is taking place, they leave a door hanger with the words "Thanks. You are making a difference." If the opposite is true, the hanger says "Gotcha. Wasted resources are gone forever."

The energy patrols in Tucson, Arizona, schools are sponsored by the Tucson Electric Power Company (TEP), which supplies the materials for monitoring—clipboards, badges, record forms, and door hangers for teams of ten to twenty students. The patrols go to classrooms, offices, and other areas during after-school hours or other times when rooms are likely to be empty. If patrols find lights on when not needed, they quickly turn them off. Periodically, they also check thermostats to see that they stay at an energy-saving temperature. They also monitor and report water leaks and, like the "Earth Patrols," leave door hangers as

Does Lawn Mowing Harm the Environment?

Anyone who has the task of lawn mowing might want to consider these statistics published by *The Week* magazine: "Americans spend more than 3 billion hours a year pushing or riding gasoline-powered lawn and garden equipment that gives off toxic exhaust and greenhouse gases. A gas-powered mower emits as much pollution per hour as 11 cars." So what is the alternative? Use a push mower? Or perhaps bring in some grazing livestock. That was the solution for school officials in Carlisle, Pennsylvania—they brought in a herd of sheep to "mow" the district's school yards, "saving $15,000 a year in landscaping costs," according to a report in *The Week*.[7]

reminders to conserve energy ("Keep it off") or to praise efforts to do so ("You're doing a great job").

TEP reports that schools in Tucson have saved millions of dollars since starting energy patrols. Schools in other states have experienced savings as well. TEP cites these examples:

- A computer left on 24 hours a day in Clark County, Nevada, wastes $224 a year in electricity. By shutting off their 60,000 computers at the end of the day, students in the Clark County School District had saved more than $1 million dollars by the end of 2002.
- Florida's Broward School District is saving $100,000 a year by replacing 40-watt lightbulbs with three-way LED bulbs in its exit signs.
- Adding an "energy monitor" to school vending machines can reduce energy costs on the machines by up to 50 percent. By installing twenty devices in six schools, Moscow School District in Idaho was able to save close to $20,000 a year.[8]

Solar and Wind Power

Solar and wind power are alternative energy sources that are eco-friendly means for generating the power needed to operate electrical appliances, heat water and buildings, and reduce greenhouse gases. These power sources can be expensive to develop, although kits to create solar panels and wind turbines are available for home use and do-it-yourself projects. Going beyond individual projects, high school students in diverse parts of the country have initiated alternative energy projects for their communities.

In Pinellas County, Florida, for example, students from the Seminole Vocational Education Center built solar-powered shelters for the homeless during their summer vacation in 2010. Pinellas Hope and Catholic Charities asked the students for help with the project. Zachery Lewis, a student at the center, reports, "We jumped on that and had all these kids come together and actually want to do this." Forty students worked on the project and built six wooden shelters with solar panels on the roof. The panels provide electricity for a light and a fan for each shelter. Teenager Evan Humphry from the center notes, "You see all these people living in tents with nothing, and then you can come here and volunteer and help build and give them a little bit of something to help make their life better."[9]

In Bellingham, Washington, two seniors, Kelli Finet and Jenessa Moore, at Nooksack Valley High School took the lead in 2010 to get their school to become part of the Cool School Challenge, a program to reduce energy use. The two girls received training in how to measure energy use in the classroom and took that information to teachers in Nooksack Valley. Moore reports, "Once we brought it to the school, the teachers got really fired up about it."[10] As a result the schools in the valley significantly reduced energy and carbon emissions.

In Oregon, students in science classes and the Earth Club at the Hood River Valley High School initiated a turbine project to make wind power work for their school. In 2009, Alice Zanmiller, who was a junior at the time, told a reporter,

"We wanted a way for people to see, to create awareness and to start the ball rolling on energy consciousness." Although there are huge wind turbines working throughout the area, some people adamantly oppose them. So the students had to convince adults in the community that the turbine "wasn't going to be real loud, and it wasn't going to kill birds," as one student puts it. After the students received approval from neighbors and the school board, a small turbine was installed with funds from Energy Trust of Oregon, which also paid for upkeep. The turbine produces enough power to operate a household and reduces the school's electricity costs, according to the news report.[11]

California teenager Adam Roudonis of Westlake Village High School founded a group in 2009 called Students for Solar Schools (SSS), which, with student leaders in various parts of the country, is prompting schools to install solar panels. Roudonis said that the idea for SSS began in middle school when he was "old enough to understand the implications of global warming and the benefits of being sustainable. Since then, I've tried to involve myself as much as I could with environmental causes, culminating with my founding of Students for Solar Schools."[12] As of 2011, the group has worked with schools in California, Oregon, New Jersey, New York, Puerto Rico, Texas, the Carolinas, Rhode Island, Missouri, Minnesota, and Virginia. In some schools solar panels have been installed successfully, and in others efforts are only in the beginning stages as students make presentations, seek grants, hold fundraisers, and create publicity materials to tout the benefits of solar energy.

In addition to working on SSS campaigns, Roudonis filed a lawsuit against the federal government in May 2011, demanding action to curb global warming. He was "part of a barrage of similar legal actions filed simultaneously in all 50 states and around the world by young plaintiffs who are directly affected by climate change." Roudonis notes, "We don't have political power. We don't have the money to compete with corporate lobbyists. We can't vote. All we have is our voice."[13]

Other Alternative Energy Sources

While wind and solar power currently are the most discussed and familiar renewable energy sources, other sources include hydroelectric power (generating energy from water sources), geothermal energy (using heat from the earth), biomass, methane gas (generated from cow manure, chicken waste, and some landfills), and wave power (energy from ocean surface waves).

Hydroelectricity is one of the oldest methods of producing power. People have used moving water to help them in their work throughout history, and currently people make great use of moving water to produce electricity. Although most energy in the United States is produced by fossil fuel and nuclear power plants, about 7 percent of total power is produced by hydroelectric plants, according to the U.S. Geological Survey. Dams, such as the Hoover Dam, contain huge power generators, and "water flowing through the dams spin turbine blades . . . which are connected to generators. Power is produced and is sent to homes and businesses."[14]

Geothermal is a term that combines the Greek *geo* for "earth" and *therine*, meaning "heat." The energy is generated in the earth's core, where temperatures hotter than the sun's surface are continuously produced by the slow decay of radioactive particles, a process that happens in all rocks. Most of the geothermal reservoirs in the United States are located in the western states and Hawaii. California generates the most electricity from geothermal energy, says the U.S. Energy Information Administration of the U.S. Department of Energy.

Wave power devices—both onshore and offshore—generate energy directly from surface waves or from pressure

? Did You Know?

Most people are aware that the Niagara Falls on the U.S. and Canadian border are one of the world's natural wonders. But the Falls also help generate some of the least expensive electricity anywhere. The United States and Canada have shared the Niagara River's water power that produces steady supplies of clean, carbon-free hydroelectricity.

These wind turbines provide an alternative source of energy.

fluctuations below the surface. Wave-power areas of the United Stares are on the northeastern and northwestern coasts. The costs of creating wave power systems are higher than systems for traditional energy, but once built, the costs for operating and maintaining them are low.

Electricity generated from biomass combustion uses conventional boilers that burn primarily waste wood. When burned, the wood waste produces steam, which is used to spin a turbine. The spinning turbine activates a generator that produces electricity. Biomass that decays in landfills also produces energy—primarily methane gas, which can be burned in a boiler to produce steam for generating electricity.[15]

These alternative energy sources are being tapped in feasible locations, many of them on Native American reservations. Tribes increasingly are "tapping power from solar and geothermal sources, and from wind, biomass, hydrogen and ocean waves," reports Linda Sikkema in *State Legislatures*. She adds, "New energy projects are popping up all around the country. The Confederated Tribes of Warm Springs in Central Oregon are on their way to becoming a major energy supplier

Increases in Alternative Sources of Energy

The Lawrence Livermore National Laboratory of the U.S. Department of Energy reports that the United States used significantly less coal and petroleum in 2009 than in 2008 and much more wind power. There also was a decline in natural gas use and increases in solar, hydro, and geothermal power.[16] British Petroleum (BP) and Royal Dutch Shell say that by 2050 one third of the world's energy will need to come from alternative energy sources. Climate change and population growth will increase the need for solar, wind, geothermal, and other renewables.[17]

in the Pacific Northwest. The tribes' own interest is in two large hydroelectric projects and a biomass project that operates on wood waste from the tribes' lumber mill. Another project in the works is a large biomass plant that will use forest waste to generate renewable electricity for more than 15,000 homes." Other tribes are involved in alternative energy projects, such as generating geothermal power on the Paiute Reservation in Nevada where

> hot springs in Pyramid Lake . . . will produce enough power for approximately 28,000 homes. Another tribe, the Makah Indian Nation in Washington, hopes to harness the ocean's power. It is working with AquaEnergy Group to construct a pilot offshore wave energy power plant. Buoys, placed some 3.2 nautical miles offshore in water depths of about 150 feet, will generate enough electricity to power 150 homes in the area.[18]

What about Nuclear Power?

Does the world need nuclear power? Since nuclear power plants do not emit greenhouse gases, is it the clean energy of the future? Should states build more nuclear power plants? What should be done with the radioactive waste from nuclear power plants? Can global warming be reduced with the use of nuclear energy? These questions and many others have been raised and debated worldwide in regard to nuclear energy as an alternative to fossil fuels.

Another issue highly debated is the safety of nuclear power. In the United States, the debate intensified in 1979 after about half of the reactor core melted at the Three-Mile Island plant in Pennsylvania. Then in 1986, a nuclear accident occurred at the Chernobyl Nuclear Power Plant in the Ukraine. Radioactive contamination spread over much of western Russia and Europe. On March 11, 2011, a 9.0 magnitude earthquake struck the island of Japan, which was followed by a tsunami. These triggered a series of ongoing equipment failures

"Teen Goes Nuclear"

The above title was a 2006 headline in the *Detroit Free Press*. The article describes the nuclear fusion reactor that teenager Thiago Olson of Oakland Township, Michigan, built in his basement. Thiago spent two years researching and building his reactor and was called a "mad scientist" by some of his friends. Currently only eighteen amateurs worldwide have created nuclear fusion. Nevertheless, the reporter describes him as modest and a "typical teenager" who said he was "always interested in science. It's always been my best subject in school."

Thiago's reactor consists of a steel chamber with the air sucked out. As the reporter explains, "Then, deuterium gas—a form of hydrogen—is injected into the vacuum. About 40,000 volts of electricity are charged into the chamber from a piece of equipment taken from an old mammogram machine. As the machine runs, the atoms in the chamber are attracted to the center and soon—ta da— nuclear fusion." After that a "small intense ball of energy forms."[19] The story about Thiago's reactor has been printed repeatedly on blogs and other Internet sites.

and subsequent release of radioactive material at the Fukushima Nuclear Power Plant maintained by the Tokyo Electric Power Company. The Japanese tragedy has created even more widespread fear over the safety of nuclear power plants. Nevertheless, proponents of nuclear energy declare that it is needed to provide affordable electricity for an increasing population. No doubt, the debate over nuclear power will continue far into the future.

Notes

1. Josh Peterson, "Teen Climate Champ Warms Schools to Solar Power," *Treehugger.com*, January 29, 2009, www.treehugger.com/files/2009/01/solar-schools-climate-champion.php (accessed May 18, 2011).

2. Ameshia Cross, "Tapping into the Energy of Teens," *Greenversations*, April 5, 2011, http://blog.epa.gov/blog/2011/04/05/energy-of-teens (accessed May 21, 2011).

3. "Consumption by the United States," *Mindfully.org*, n.d., www.mindfully.org/Sustainability/Americans-Consume-24percent.htm (accessed October 22, 2011).

4. *SmartPowerEd*, n.d., http://smartpowered.org (accessed May 23, 2011).

5. Lauri Vaughan, "Harker Trio Gangs Up on Global Warming," *Harker News*, April 2010, http://news.harker.org/harker-trio-gangs-up-on-global-warming (accessed May 23, 2011).

6. Tennessee Pollution Prevention Partnership Success Story, "Douglass High School Saves Energy," February 2011, http://tn.gov/environment/ea/tp3/docs/tp3_ss-douglasshs_11ec.pdf (accessed May 17, 2011).

7. "Blades of Glory," *The Week*, July 1–8, 2011, p. 11.

8. Tucson Electric Power, *The Energy Patrol Teacher's Manual*, 2002, p. 4.

9. Leigh Spann, "Handy Pinellas Teens Build Solar Shelters for Homeless," *News Channel 8*, July 13, 2010, http://suncoastpinellas.tbo.com/content/2010/jul/13/handy-pinellas-teens-build-solar-shelters-homeless/news/?utm_source=feedburner&utm_medium=feed&utm_campaign=Feed%3A+tbo%2Fpinellas+%28TBO+%3E+Pinellas%29&utm_content=Google+Reader (accessed May 17, 2011).

10. Dean Kahn, "Nooksack Valley Teens Energetically Reduce School's Energy Use," *bellinghamherald.com*, September 2, 2010, www.bellinghamherald.com/2010/09/02/v-print/1595555/nooksack-valley-teens-energetically.html (accessed May 19, 2011).

11. Shelby Wood, "Campus Turbine Gives Hood River Teens the (Wind) Power," *The Oregonian*, January 29, 2009, www.oregonlive.com/environment/index.ssf/2009/01/hood_river_teens_get_the_wind.html (accessed May 17, 2011).

12. Josh Peterson, "Teen Climate Champ Warms Schools to Solar Power," *Treehugger.com*, January 29, 2009, www.treehugger.com/files/2009/01/solar-schools-climate-champion.php (accessed May 18, 2011).

13. Marya Jones Barlow, "Teen Activist Plans 'Million Kid March' to Fight Global Warming," *Ventura County Star*, May 4, 2011, www.vcstar.com/news/2011/may/04/teen-activist-plans-145million-kid-march-to (accessed May 18, 2011).

14. U.S. Department of Interior, U.S. Geological Survey, "Hydroelectric Power Water Use," February 8, 2011, http://ga.water.usgs.gov/edu/wuhy.html (accessed May 22, 2011).

15. U.S. Department of Energy, "Energy Savers," February 9, 2011, www.energysavers.gov/renewable_energy (accessed May 23, 2011).

16. Lawrence Livermore National Laboratory. "Americans Using Less Energy, More Renewables," news release, August 23, 2010, www.llnl.gov/news/newsreleases/2010/NR-10-08-05.html (accessed November 8, 2011).

17. Alternative Energy, n.d., www.altenergy.org/ (accessed November 8, 2011).

18. Linda Sikkema, "Native American Power: Native American Tribes Are Tapping into Alternative Energy Sources with Great Benefits to Themselves and Their Neighbors," *State Legislatures*, June 1, 2007, www.thefreelibrary.com/Native+American+power:+Native+American+tribes+are+tapping+into...-a0164423356 (accessed May 22, 2011).

19. Gina Damron, "Teen Goes Nuclear: He Creates Fusion in His Oakland Township Home," *Detroit Free Press*, November 19, 2006, http://research.lifeboat.com/teen.goes.nuclear.htm (accessed May 22, 2011).

GETTING THERE THE GREEN WAY

"I like to talk about our biodiesel program to make fuel out of used vegetable oil—how it works and why it's better for the environment."
—Michelle Patzelt, a member of a high school science club who gives presentations to various schools on how to be green[1]

Katherine Schultz was a new teenage driver in 2010, taking classes at a New Canaan, Connecticut, driving school, where she learned about "brakes and safety in the car." But there were no instructions about eco-friendly driving. She notes, "We hear all the time about pollution and how your car affects global warming, but we didn't learn that."[2] With the support of the state's Department of Motor Vehicles, Katherine created a short film for teens titled *From Teen Driver to Green Driver*. The film was shown for a time on the DMV's website, and it included tips for green driving, such as keeping tires inflated properly, not idling the car for more than a minute when possible, planning errands to make fewer stops, and keeping the engine tuned. Another suggestion was to shop for an affordable fuel-efficient vehicle. That could be a hybrid car that uses two types of energy, electricity and diesel fuel; however hybrids are more expensive than conventional cars. Or perhaps it is a vehicle that uses biofuel.

Biofuels

Whatever and wherever energy projects are under way, biofuels are on the front burner, so to speak. The term refers to any solid, liquid, or gas fuel made from the decay of biological materials, such as algae, corn, sugarcane, soybeans, switchgrass, sorghum, discarded foods, waste cooking oils, and animal waste. To date, the biofuels being produced in the United States are bioethanol distilled from ethyl alcohol and biodiesel. According to Professor Michael E. Salassi in the Department of Agricultural Economics and Agribusiness, Louisiana State University, "Ethanol (ethyl alcohol) is produced from petrochemical feedstocks, such as ethylene, and is also produced biologically by fermenting sugars with yeast. Diesel is commonly made as a distillate from petroleum fuel oil. Both of these fuels, however, can be produced from biological feedstocks, hence the terms bioethanol and biodiesel."[3]

Companies producing biodiesel are appearing in many states. In addition, high school and college students are experimenting with the production of biodiesel. Students in a chemistry class at Newton North High School near Boston, Massachusetts, for example, are distilling biodiesel fuel from their cafeteria's food waste and throw-away food from local restaurants. The students also are experimenting with algae-based fuel.

Consider also a project undertaken by students at Whitney Young School in Chicago. The high school students are members of a club called HEROES (Helping to Engender Renewable Organic Energy Sources). They have worked in the laboratory at Northwestern University to make biodiesel from waste oil contributed by local restaurants. Their refinery started with student Anna Hernandez, who received help from one of her teachers to create biodiesel for a science fair project. That idea expanded to the development of two refineries, one of which was donated to a school in Mendota, Illinois. The students also have redesigned a city bus so that it can be fueled on biodiesel and used to transport foods for Food Desert, a program that operates an urban mobile market that takes fresh produce to neighborhoods that do not have major grocery stores and instead have only convenience stores and fast-food restaurants. One of the members of HEROES notes, "We spent four days helping [Food Desert] dismantle the bus and put it back together." Another student remarks that working on the project made

It Happened to New Jersey Teens

Four New Jersey teenagers took on an experiment to produce microalgae that could be used to make biodiesel fuel, a renewable alternative with less toxic emissions than fossil fuels like petroleum. The students were twin sisters Eliana and Ariella Applebaum, their friend Elana Forman (all from Ma'ayanot Yeshiva High School for Girls), and Elana's brother, Yakir (from Torah Academy of Bergen County). According to a news report, the group "developed a system for growing algae and converting it into fuel that has produced the first-ever 100 percent algae-based fuel to be used in a home heater." (A combination of algae fuel and petroleum has been used previously as a power source.) How did the teenagers do it? According to an article in the *Jewish Standard*, "They grew the algae in Snapple bottles, using fluorescent lights and air valves connected to carbon dioxide pumps, and added nutrients. They then filtered the algae, using cheesecloth, filter paper, and buckets." In the end, the algae was converted to biofuel that burned successfully. Eliana reports, "It was rewarding to see what we could produce on our own—how it could affect the environment and make a difference in the world."[4]

her "want to do bigger things. I plan on going into science." A third HEROES member declares that the project "provided a real incentive for me to continue research in general concerning environmentally friendly programs."[5]

Another possible alternative fuel is ammonia, a compound of nitrogen and hydrogen (NH_3), which does not produce greenhouse gases when burned. During World War II, ammonia was substituted for gasoline and diesel in Belgium to fuel buses because regular fuels were not available. Vehicles could be modified to run on what is known as anhydrous NH_3, but to create this fuel, large amounts of CO_2 are produced, doing little to reduce the carbon footprint. However, the "solution according to the companies developing NH_3 as a transportation fuel is to use

Pros and Cons of Biofuels

Whatever the source for creating biofuels, there are some pros and cons. First, the advantages: Biofuels cost less to produce than fossil fuels, and they can be refined from a variety of renewable materials as well as from recycled waste. Production of biofuels provides jobs and is safer than petroleum to clean up if spilled. When used as an energy source, biofuels emit less carbon and toxic pollution than oil and gasoline.

The drawbacks of biofuels include a low energy output compared to traditional fuels, which means that larger amounts of biofuels are required to equal the energy produced from oil and gas. While biofuels burn cleaner than traditional fuels, planting crops and building the plants to make biofuel produce high levels of carbon dioxide emissions. In addition, forests are cleared in some countries to produce crops like corn, soybeans, and palm oil for biofuel; deforestation greatly increases carbon emissions. Because food crops are grown in some places to produce biofuels, the cost of food can increase. Finally, biofuels and vehicles that use this alternative source are not yet available on a large scale.

excess electricity and renewable energy sources like wind power to split water to get the hydrogen to use in the creation of ammonia," according to a report in the *Vancouver Green Transportation Examiner*.[6]

"Grease Cars"

Imagine going to a restaurant to scavenge for discarded fry oil, then using it to fuel your car or truck. An increasing number of vehicle owners are doing just that. The exhaust from their cars or trucks may smell like French fries or Chinese or Mexican food or maybe even salad dressing. The vehicles are called "grease cars" or "veggie cars" because owners have converted them to run on throw-away grease from restaurants or on straight vegetable oil (SVO). This is an alternative fuel that, in the case of throw-away grease, is free for the asking. Veggie fuels are also eco-friendly—they are biodegradable, renewable, nontoxic, and reduce greenhouse gas emissions.

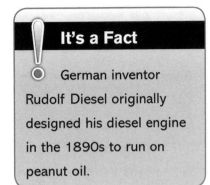

It's a Fact

German inventor Rudolf Diesel originally designed his diesel engine in the 1890s to run on peanut oil.

To use throw-away grease as an alternative fuel, vehicles must have diesel engines, which can be converted to use some diesel fuel along with the used cooking oil. Here is how Tom and Ray (Click and Clack) of the radio show *Car Talk* explain the conversion:

> There's a tank for regular diesel fuel, for starting the car, and a second tank for the vegetable oil. This second tank contains a metal coil that transfers heat from the engine's coolant. The driver starts the car on diesel fuel and can only switch over to vegetable oil when the veggie oil has warmed up enough. Before you turn the engine off, you must switch back to regular diesel and run the vehicle long enough to purge the fuel lines and injectors of the vegetable oil. Otherwise, the lines will get clogged and it'll be a whole lot of work if you ever want to get your vehicle started again.[7]

No modification is necessary for vehicles that use biodiesel, which is a mixture of 80 to 90 percent diesel fuel and 10 to 20 percent vegetable oil, called B10 or B20. Biodiesel is just one type of biofuel being produced for those who want alternatives to petroleum-based products.

Green Driving

Dozens of websites have eco-friendly driving guidelines. One of them is the Green Car Institute (greencars.org), which has posted green driving tips that are

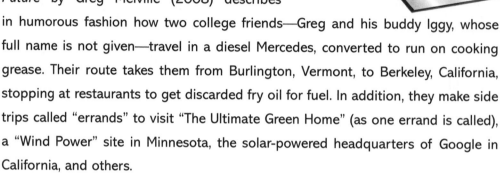

From the Bookshelf

Greasy Rider: Two Dudes, One Fry-Oil-Powered Car, and a Cross-Country Search for a Greener Future by Greg Melville (2008) describes in humorous fashion how two college friends—Greg and his buddy Iggy, whose full name is not given—travel in a diesel Mercedes, converted to run on cooking grease. Their route takes them from Burlington, Vermont, to Berkeley, California, stopping at restaurants to get discarded fry oil for fuel. In addition, they make side trips called "errands" to visit "The Ultimate Green Home" (as one errand is called), a "Wind Power" site in Minnesota, the solar-powered headquarters of Google in California, and others.

included in the American Council for an Energy-Efficient Economy's (ACEEE's) Green Book Online. Here are some of the ACEEE's suggestions (reprinted with permission):

- Avoid "jack rabbit" starts and aggressive driving. Flooring the gas pedal not only wastes gas, it leads to drastically higher pollution rates.
- Try to anticipate stops and let your vehicle coast down as much as possible.
- Avoid the increased pollution, wasted gas, and wear on your brakes created by accelerating hard and braking hard.
- Follow the speed limit! Driving 75 mph instead of 65 mph will lower your fuel economy by about 10 percent, and can dramatically increase tailpipe pollution in many vehicles.
- Combine trips. Warmed-up engines and catalysts generate much less air pollution, so combining several short trips into one can make a big difference.
- Take a few moments to unload your cargo area. Carrying around an extra 100 pounds reduces fuel economy by about 1 percent.

- Try using the vents and opening windows to cool off before you turn on the air conditioner. Air conditioner use increases fuel consumption, increases emissions in some vehicles, and involves environmentally damaging fluids.
- Keep your tires properly inflated. Tires should be inflated to the pressure recommended for your vehicle; this information is often printed inside the door frame or in your owner's manual. For every three pounds below recommended pressure, fuel economy goes down by about 1 percent.
- Get a tune-up. Whether you do it yourself or go to a mechanic, a tune-up can increase your fuel economy. Follow owner's manual guidelines. Be sure to check for worn spark plugs, dragging brakes, and low transmission fluid; have your wheels aligned and tires rotated; and replace the air filter if needed. Make sure all used vehicle fluids are recycled or disposed of safely.
- Change the oil. In addition to making your car or truck last longer, replacing the oil and oil filter regularly will also help fuel economy.
- Have your vehicle's emission control system checked periodically. Take it in for service if an instrument panel warning light comes on.
- Park in the shade in summer to keep your car cool and minimize evaporation of fuel.
- If you have a garage, use it as much as possible to keep your car warm in winter and cool in summer.
- If you have to park outdoors, windshield shades can cut down on summer heat and help keep the frost off in the winter.[8]

One more way to be a green driver is to share a ride by carpooling or vanpooling. Whether going to work or school, people who need a ride can find many online sources available to contact drivers who will take along passengers. Drivers also can be matched with people seeking a ride. Many colleges and universities have carpool programs that provide special reserved parking with a valid permit. Some have opted for software that allows students to connect to an online ride-sharing program operated by a nonuniversity company. One of the most recent is Zimride, initiated in 2007 at Cornell University in Ithaca, New York. Since then dozens of universities have signed up for the program, including University of California, Los Angeles; Stanford University in Menlo Park, California; University of Michigan in Ann Arbor; Eastern Kentucky University in Richmond; and Dartmouth College in Hanover, New Hampshire. At Indiana University in Bloomington, where the program was initiated in 2010, the *Indiana Daily Student* explains that the service

> combines Google Maps, Facebook, Twitter and customer reviews to link drivers with potential riders. . . . After creating an account through the University Central Authentication Service login, users can link their profiles to Facebook and post or look for upcoming trips. . . . A Google Maps interface shows the exact route planned by the driver seeking a rider to split costs or the desired route for a rider seeking a driver. Once users have finished sharing a ride they can rate their riding partners. . . . [And] each user's . . . profile displays the amount of carbon emissions reduced by sharing a ride through Zimride.[9]

The ratings are an important part of the program because they provide credibility. In the past, some carpools have not worked well because they were not dependable or students did not know the drivers and riders, and that caused some friction.

Walking, Biking, and Using Public Transportation

You can talk the talk, but can you walk the walk? Someone who advocates living green should be able to not only talk about it but also to walk the walk. When it comes to getting there the green way, how about walking to a destination whenever possible? Or riding a bicycle? Or roller skating? Or skate boarding? Or taking public transportation, including the school bus?

Walking certainly is the oldest form of transportation; it has been a way to get from one place to another ever since humans became upright. Some people

Riding a bicycle to school or the store or to do errands is one way to travel green.

call walking the "ankle express," and many cities across the United States are attempting to find ways for people to walk safely to school, work, restaurants, entertainment spots, parks, and other areas. Walking not only is eco-friendly, but it also is healthy—good for the heart, weight loss, and even mental and spiritual stimulation. And it is free.

Along with walking, riding a bike is a green way to travel, especially if you use pedal power. To encourage biking, U.S. secretary of transportation Ray LaHood began using a bicycle in 2011 to get around Washington, D.C. He encourages people to use that form of transportation to conserve energy as well as to get exercise.

Some U.S. cities, such as Washington, D.C.; Minneapolis, Minnesota; Denver, Colorado; Boston, Massachusetts; and others, have established bike sharing or smart biking programs that are designed for short-term bicycle use in urban areas. A bicyclist must first buy a membership in the network for a modest fee and then using a smart card or credit card can borrow a bike at a station and drop it off at another kiosk near his or her destination. In Washington, D.C., the Capital Bikeshare program has more than 10,700 members who make about 3,000 trips each day. According to a *Washington Post* article, membership in the D.C. program "costs $75 for a year, $25 for a month, $15 for five days and $5 for 24 hours. Long-term members get a key to unlock a bike from the docking station; short-term members get a five-digit code for the same task. The first 30 minutes of riding are free. Fees kick in after that until the bike is returned to another docking station."[10] Bikes at kiosks or docks may be identified by bright blue, red, yellow, or green colors. Bicyclists are responsible for returning their two-wheelers. Although there have been concerns about thefts from the kiosks, only rarely are bikes stolen from the docks and that usually is because someone has used a stolen credit card to "borrow" a bike and keep it. The programs have become so popular that 2011 was a year of smart biking startups in one U.S. city after another.

While many people rent bikes to do errands, they also use them to get to public transportation centers, where they can return the bikes and get on a bus, train, or subway to go to school or work. Bike owners also are able to integrate their bicycle travel with public transit through bike-and-ride programs in which bikes are stored at stations until owners return to pick them up. Bikes also can travel along on exterior racks or hooks on public buses and are allowed in holding areas of some commuter trains and light rail during nonpeak travel times. According to a study published in the *Journal of Public Transportation*, "with the second largest transit system in the U.S., Chicago has made impressive efforts to integrate cycling with public transport. Its special distinction lies in the innovative provision of bike parking at rail stations, tailoring the design of parking facilities to each station's particular situation. . . . There are 2,153 bike parking spaces at 131 of the 143 CTA subway and elevated rail stations and 4,267 spaces at 50 of the 76 Metra suburban rail stations. Moreover, indoor or sheltered parking is available at 83 CTA stations, more than any other transit system in North America. The specific location of bike racks inside the stations provides both weather protection and greater security, since they are usually placed within easy sight of station attendants and other passengers."[12]

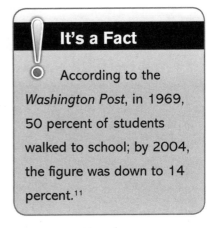

It's a Fact

According to the *Washington Post*, in 1969, 50 percent of students walked to school; by 2004, the figure was down to 14 percent.[11]

Bicycle Safety

"Teen Bicyclist Dies after Hit by Car"

"Teenage Bicyclist Injured by Car in South Pasadena"

"Teen Bicyclist Killed in Madison County"

"Teen Bicyclist Killed by Hit-and-Run Driver in Canoga Park"

"Young Driver Crashes into Teen Bicyclist, Skateboarder"

"Teen Bicyclist Injured in Land Park, Sacramento"

"Teen Bicyclist Collides with Car on Pleasant Home Road, Augusta, Georgia"

These are just a smattering of headlines posted on the Internet in the spring of 2011. As the use of bicycles increases nationwide—sometimes because of green advocacy—safety of riders is a major concern, which often translates into creating bike paths or bike lanes in many cities. But accidents still happen, sometimes because of careless or drunk drivers and sometimes because bicyclists are not alert or do not take safety precautions. The National Highway Traffic Safety Administration (NHTSA) of the U.S. Department of Transportation keeps statistics on nonmotorized bicycle, tricycle, and unicycle (lumped together as

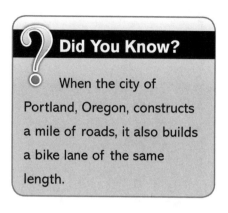

Did You Know?

When the city of Portland, Oregon, constructs a mile of roads, it also builds a bike lane of the same length.

pedacycle) fatalities, which in 2009 (the latest figure) was 630 deaths. Twenty thousand bicyclists ages sixteen to thirty-four were injured and 168 killed in 2009. In 2009, the average age of pedalcyclists killed in traffic crashes was forty-one. The top states with pedacycle fatalities are Florida with 107 deaths, California with 99, and Texas with 48. To prevent deaths and injuries, NHTSA has posted the following on its website:

Important Safety Reminders

- All bicyclists should wear properly fitted bicycle helmets every time they ride. A helmet is the single most effective way to prevent head injury resulting from a bicycle crash.
- Bicyclists are considered vehicle operators; they are required to obey the same rules of the road as other vehicle operators, including obeying traffic signs, signals, and lane markings. When cycling in the street, cyclists must ride in the same direction as traffic.
- Drivers of motor vehicles need to share the road with bicyclists. Be courteous—allow at least three feet clearance when passing a bicyclist on the road, look for cyclists before opening a car door or pulling out from a parking space, and yield to cyclists at intersections and as directed by signs and signals. Be especially watchful for cyclists when making turns, either left or right.
- Bicyclists should increase their visibility to drivers by wearing fluorescent or brightly colored clothing during the day, dawn, and dusk. To be noticed when riding at night, use a front light and a red reflector or flashing rear light, and use retro-reflective tape or markings on equipment or clothing.[13]

Bicycling Ambassadors

In Chicago, Illinois, a team of teenagers has been working since 2000 with the city's Bicycling Ambassadors to talk to younger children about bicycle safety. Called Junior Ambassadors, the teenagers work from late June through early August, primarily at day camps. High-schoolers who want to be junior ambassadors complete an after-school bicycle safety and repair class. The ten-week course is sponsored by "After School Matters, a not-for-profit agency that offers Chicago teenagers an opportunity to learn job skills and apply those skills at different summer jobs. The Junior Ambassador program is the only peer-to-peer education program of its kind."[14]

In 2010, the ambassadors educated nearly 60,000 people about bicycle safety. In some instances they stopped cyclists who ran traffic lights and stop signs to explain bicycle laws and to encourage them to stay off sidewalks. They also provided cyclists a white front headlight for their bikes if they did not have one. In addition they distributed hundreds of free helmets to young bike riders and made sure the helmets fit properly.

Future Green Transportation

Will the means of transportation become more eco-friendly in the years ahead? That question is being addressed by a variety of experts in the United States and other countries. In Britain, Motor Development International has developed a three-wheeled vehicle called the AirPod, which runs on compressed air. The company hopes the vehicle will be used for future transport in urban areas. In 2011, the first solar-powered airplane flew around the globe, and that plane could be a model for the future. A green taxi system has been designed that could be a future means of urban transport. It is a cabinlike vehicle that has solar panels on its roof to supply the electricity to power its engine. Several cabins can be linked together like a train for travel.

A futurist energy source may be developed in some countries on the basis of Tokyo's subway system, which is used by millions. At the busiest stations, the Japanese government has installed flooring tiles that generate electricity. The tiles are in front of ticket turnstiles, and as people walk through, the tiles capture energy, which is "stored in capacitors and channeled to the station's ticket gates and electric lights and displays."[15]

Beyond such innovations, future transportation will no doubt include some U.S. policy changes to require higher fuel efficiency—more miles per gallon for vehicles. There also will be an increase in stations to recharge electric vehicle batteries. Airplanes will be developed to make use of new designs to improve fuel consumption.

The demand for oil as fuel probably will decrease, although in the United States that will depend on subsidies for alternative fuel production. Rapid rail transport will be a priority for many parts of the United States, but some states—especially Florida—have refused to take advantage of federal subsidies for development of high-speed rail, which prompted groups of Floridians in 2011 to protest strongly.

Notes

1. "The Voice of a Green Generation," *Knowledge@Wharton High School*, April 22, 2011, http://kwhs.wharton.upenn.edu/2011/04/the-voice-of-a-green-generation (accessed May 25, 2011).
2. Brittany Lyte, "From Teen Driver to Green Driver: A Fledgling Motorist Promotes Eco-Friendly Practices," *New Canaan News*, February 11, 2010, www.newcanaannewsonline.com/news/article/From-teen-driver-to-green-driver-a-fledgling-360288.php (accessed May 24, 2011).
3. Michael E. Salassi, "Current Status U.S. Biofuel Industry," *LSU Ag Center*, January 2009 (updated January 2011), www.lsuagcenter.com/NR/rdonlyres/BC29EC77-DD79-41CC-9FD9-AD84541C41C1/54004/BiofuelIndustryFactSheet.pdf (accessed May 21, 2011).
4. Heather Robinson, "Teens Channel Energies into Alternative Energy," *Jewish Standard*, March 25, 2011, p. 9.
5. Sarah Moore, "HEROES," *Medill Reports*, April 27, 2011, http://news.medill.northwestern.edu/chicago/news.aspx?id=185486 (accessed May 21, 2011).
6. Michael Grey, "Will Ammonia Be the Transportation Fuel of the Future?" *Vancouver Green Transportation Examiner*, January 28, 2011, www.examiner.com/green-transportation-in-vancouver/will-ammonia-be-the-transportation-fuel-of-the-future? (accessed July 8, 2011).

7. Car Talk, "Vegetable Oil," n.d., www.cartalk.com/content/features/alternativefuels/vegetableoil.html (accessed May 24, 2011).

8. American Council for an Energy-Efficient Economy, "Green Driving Tips," *Greencars.org*, n.d., www.greenercars.org/drivingtips.htm (accessed May 25, 2011).

9. Claire Wiseman, "Zimride Shares Rides to Cut Emissions, Costs," *Indiana Daily Student*, April 21, 2010, www.idsnews.com/news/story.aspx?id=75421 (accessed May 27, 2011).

10. Ashley Halsey III, "Spring Brings Growth of Regional Public Bicycle Program Capital Bikeshare," *Washington Post*, April 23, 2011, www.washingtonpost.com/local/commuting/spring-brings-growth-of-regional-bike-sharing-program/2011/04/21/AFFd8EXE_story.html (accessed May 26, 2011).

11. Neil Peirce, "Biking and Walking—Our Secret Weapon?" *Washington Post*, July 19, 2009, http://citiwire.net/post/1125 (accessed May 26, 2011).

12. John Pucher and Ralph Buehler, "Integrating Bicycling and Public Transit in North America," *Journal of Public Transportation*, vol. 12, no. 3, 2009, pp. 91–92, www.nctr.usf.edu/jpt/pdf/JPT12-3Pucher.pdf (accessed May 26, 2011).

13. U.S. Department of Transportation, National Highway Traffic Safety Administration, "Traffic Safety Facts 2009 Data," www-nrd.nhtsa.dot.gov/pubs/811386.pdf (accessed May 26, 2011).

14. "About the Bicycling Ambassadors," *City of Chicago's Bicycling Ambassadors*, n.d., www.bicyclingambassadors.org/about.html (accessed May 26, 2011).

15. Green Chip Living, "The Strange Future of Public Transit," *Green Chip Stocks*, February 17, 2011, www.greenchipstocks.com/articles/top-10-bizarre-public-transportation-ideas/1252 (accessed July 8, 2011).

FIGHTING FOR ENVIRONMENTAL JUSTICE

"There's this thing that nobody even knows about or talks about, really, called 'environmental racism,' where there's a disproportionate amount of pollution that's concentrated in these low-income communities of color. And it's an injustice at the level of where the air you breathe is not even clean enough for you to sustain a healthy life."
—Ryan Perez, a Latino youth speaking for his peers in
a news broadcast about a pollution protest in Vernon, Texas[1]

"In the Bayview district where minorities live, they are targeted the most with pollution and many of the people who live there don't even know it," says eighteen-year-old Ingried Seyundo, a youth organizer with People Organizing to Demand Environmental and Economic Rights (PODER). The district she mentions includes five communities in San Francisco: Bayview Hunter's Point, Portola, Excelsior, Visitation Valley, and Mission. Seyundo spoke at a week-long 2010 U.S. Social Forum in Detroit, Michigan, where a workshop was titled "Pollution Has No Borders: Black, Chinese and Latino Youth Organizing for Environmental Justice in San Francisco." Eighteen-year-old Tiffany Ng of the Common Roots Program of the Chinese Progressive Association of San Francisco (CPAS) concurs. She notes, "It is important for us to educate ourselves about these environmental issues." For her group, it was a campaign "against trucks running in residential areas. . . . We created truck routes that now allow these trucks to drive away from places where there are lots of children, like schools, and also where the elderly live."[2]

An issue for teenager Loreen Dangerfield is a plan by a Florida development company to build condominiums at the Hunter's Point Naval Shipyard. According to Dangerfield, "The shipyard itself is toxic and it's a landfill." In addition, she notes that in Miami, Florida, the company "built houses on top of undetonated bombs and people started getting sick."[3]

The concerns that these teenagers expressed at the forum have been reiterated many times since the 1980s, when people of color began protesting discriminatory environmental practices, such as dumping toxic materials and constructing municipal waste facilities and toxic chemical plants in their communities. The fight has been a long one and historically relates to the civil rights and environmental movements of the 1960s and 1970s that laid the foundation for protests against environmental racism and formation of what is called the environmental justice movement.

History of the Environmental Justice Movement

Long before *environmental racism* and *environmental justice* were coined, Native Americans were fighting for ecological justice as European colonists took over their lands—usually by force. When U.S. president Franklin Pierce asked to buy land from the Duwamish/Suquamish tribe in 1855, Chief Seattle responded that the request was strange to him and his people because

> we do not own the freshness of the air or the sparkle of the water. How can you buy them from us? Every part of this earth is sacred to my people. Every shining pine needle, every sandy shore, every mist in the dark woods, every clearing and humming insect is holy in the memory and experience of my people. We know that the white man does not understand our ways. One portion of the land is the same to him as the next, for he is a stranger who comes in the night and takes from the land whatever he needs. The earth is not his brother, but his enemy, and when he has conquered it, he moves on. His appetite will devour the earth and leave behind only a desert.[4]

When the civil rights movement was in full swing in the 1960s and 1970s, the modern environmental movement also sprouted, focusing much public attention on America's filthy waterways, polluted air, and littered landscapes. Although the civil rights and environmental movements had many common interests and concerns, their agendas seldom merged. For example, some environmentalists gave top priority to saving natural habitats and wildlife for recreational use and to preserving the beauty of nature. But people of color long had been barred by local laws or customs from many public parks, beaches, and other natural areas, so they hardly were inclined to join in conservation programs. Civil rights groups were concerned with achieving basic constitutional rights and overturning discriminatory laws and practices. Many people of color and the poor also had to worry about survival—finding and keeping jobs.

American industry and politicians also have played a part in creating divisions between environmental and civil rights groups. Frequently companies guilty of causing pollution have fought environmental regulations by claiming that jobs would be lost if the industries had to meet environmental standards. Because low-income people, whatever their ethnic background, would be most hurt by the job losses, company representatives and politicians could easily convince workers that environmentalists were to blame for factory layoffs and even for plant closings.

By 1982, a protest erupted in North Carolina over the citing of a chemical landfill, which included cancer-causing polychlorinated biphenyls (PCBs), atop a groundwater source in Warren County. Dr. Benjamin Chavis, then director of the United Church of Christ's Commission for Racial Justice (CRJ), and other black leaders took part in the protest, which led Chavis to coin the phrase *environmental racism*. Although the protest did not stop the landfill, it caught the attention of national civil rights leaders and environmentalists. It also prompted the CRJ to examine the correlation between race and toxic waste, and in 1987, the commission published its findings in *Toxic Wastes and Race in the United States: A National Report on the Racial and Social Economic Characteristics of Communities of Hazardous Waste Sites*. The study identified where toxic waste sites were located

Principles of Environmental Justice

In a condensed version, the principles of environmental justice:

- affirm the sacredness of Mother Earth, ecological unity, and the interdependence of all species and the right to be free from ecological destruction
- demand that public policy be based on mutual respect and justice for all peoples, free from any form of discrimination or bias
- mandate the right to ethical, balanced, and responsible uses of land and renewable resources in the interest of a sustainable planet for humans and other living things
- call for universal protection from nuclear testing, extraction, production, and disposal of toxic/hazardous wastes and poisons and nuclear testing that threaten the fundamental right to clean air, land, water, and food
- affirm the fundamental right to political, economic, cultural, and environmental self-determination of all peoples
- demand the cessation of the production of all toxins, hazardous wastes, and radioactive materials, and that all past and current producers be held strictly accountable to the people for detoxification and the containment at the point of production
- demand the right to participate as equal partners at every level of decision making, including needs assessment, planning, implementation, enforcement, and evaluation
- affirm the right of all workers to a safe and healthy work environment without being forced to choose between an unsafe livelihood and unemployment; also affirm the right of those who work at home to be free from environmental hazards
- protect the right of victims of environmental injustice to receive full compensation and reparations for damages as well as quality health care
- consider governmental acts of environmental injustice a violation of international law, the Universal Declaration on Human Rights, and the United Nations Convention on Genocide

- must recognize a special legal and natural relationship of native peoples to the U.S. government through treaties, agreements, compacts, and covenants affirming sovereignty and self-determination
- affirm the need for urban and rural ecological policies to clean up and rebuild our cities and rural areas in balance with nature, honoring the cultural integrity of all our communities, and provide fair access for all to the full range of resources
- call for the strict enforcement of principles of informed consent and a halt to the testing of experimental reproductive and medical procedures and vaccinations on people of color
- oppose the destructive operations of multinational corporations
- oppose military occupation, repression, and exploitation of lands, peoples, cultures, and other life forms
- call for the education of present and future generations that emphasizes social and environmental issues based on our experience and an appreciation of our diverse cultural perspectives
- require that we, as individuals, make personal and consumer choices to consume as little of Mother Earth's resources and to produce as little waste as possible and make the conscious decision to challenge and reprioritize our lifestyles to ensure the health of the natural world for present and future generations

across the United States. There was no question that toxic waste was more likely to be dumped in communities of color, especially African American and Hispanic communities as well as on Native American reservations.

Sociology professor Robert Bullard addressed the reality of environmental racism in his book *Dumping in Dixie: Race, Class and Environmental Quality* (1990). He went on to help bring about the First National People of Color Environmental Leadership Summit in 1991 held on Capitol Hill in Washington, D.C. Out of the summit came seventeen principles of environmental justice, now considered the founding document of the environmental justice movement.

By 2007, another report was prepared for the CRJ called *Toxic Wastes and Race at Twenty: 1987–2007*, which concludes that

"What Are Toxic Tours?"

In cities across the United States, environmental justice efforts often include toxic tours. The Sierra Club, an environmental organization, publishes an environmental justice newsletter, *EJ Times*, which in a 2001 issue features explanations and purposes of toxic tours. Here is their response to the question "What are toxic tours?":

> Generally, toxic tours are noncommercial visits organized and facilitated by people who reside in areas that are polluted by toxics, places that sociologist and environmental justice activist Robert D. Bullard has named "human sacrifice zones." Residents of these areas guide outsiders, or "tourists," through where they live, work, and play in order to raise awareness of their suffering and to gain support in their efforts to achieve redress. Like other environmental advocacy tours, therefore, toxic tours provide an occasion for community members to invite people (who they believe either directly or indirectly have the power to alter their environment) to better appreciate the value, and thus the fate of their environment.[5]

race continues to be an independent predictor of where hazardous wastes are located, and it is a stronger predictor than income, education and other socioeconomic indicators. . . . People of color now comprise a majority in neighborhoods with commercial hazardous waste facilities, and much larger (more than two-thirds) majorities can be found in neighborhoods with clustered facilities. People of color in 2007 are more concentrated in areas with commercial hazardous sites than in 1987. African Americans, Hispanics/Latinos, and Asian Americans/Pacific Islanders alike are disproportionately burdened by hazardous wastes in the United States.[6]

Youth Fighting for Environmental Justice

Many young people take part in toxic tours and other efforts to fight environmental racism. The year 2007 marked a triumph for an environmental youth group fighting toxic waste in East Palo Alto, California. Called Youth United for Community Action (YUCA), the group began operation in 1994 to place young people in California cities to work on environmental justice campaigns. Some of the youth went to East Palo Alto, where Romic Environmental Technologies was located and recycling hazardous materials—solvents, inks, acids, and other dangerous chemicals that are involved in the production of computer parts. The company appeared to be a green business but was instead a toxic waste site that some believed was responsible for a high incidence of cancer in the community. It was also an eyesore, with huge towers spewing chemicals. For fourteen years YUCA campaigned to shut down the Romic plant, and in 2007, the state's Department of Toxic Substances Control finally ordered the plant closed.

When asked whether YUCA would continue to operate, Charisse Domingo, who has worked with the organization since she was twenty-one years old, responds, "YUCA is always going to be about East Palo Alto first. However, we know that we are linked to the larger Environmental Justice movement in the Bay Area and to the youth-based Environmental Justice networks in the Central Valley." The organization also has been conducting toxic tours, taking various student groups and others studying environmental justice issues on tours through their community and conducting classes on what it means to fight for justice.[7]

Toxic tours also take place in the Little Village area of southwest Chicago, Illinois, with about 95,000 residents who are primarily of Mexican descent. Teen activists are involved in the Little Village Environmental Justice Organization (LVEJO), which uses its toxic tours to educate participants about the impacts of environmental racism. Marisol Becerra, who grew up in Little Village, took the toxic tour with her mother when she was a youngster. For the first time, she became aware of a coal-fired power plant that emits so much smoke she thought it was a "cloud factory." As a young teenager in 2003, Becerra joined LVEJO and learned that "several of the plant's pollutants lead to health risks such as respiratory problems, premature birth and premature death." In 2009, she was a sophomore at DePaul University in Chicago and says she was "working on a B.A. in public policy studies with an environmental policy focus. . . . Education and research are my top priorities. I aspire to obtain a Ph.D. in environmental policy from Yale University and contribute to academia as well as to my community. Ideally, I would like to be administrator of the Environmental Protection Agency."[8]

Other teenagers in Little Village also advocate for clean power sources and a park. As Carolina, one of the teen activists, told *Emagazine*, "Anywhere you go [in Little Village], you'll face chemicals, contaminated soil, air pollution, traffic, diesel trucks everywhere. When I come out of school, I feel the air so thick with diesel fumes. Anywhere you go in Little Village, you'll face an environmental justice hazard. The biggest community victory has been Little Village–Lawndale High School." Although the school and a park are being built on a toxic site, the land will be cleaned up, which the teenagers consider a victory. In Carolina's view, "We are the ones who are going to be in that environment, at the park, at the school. We are the ones who'd really like to have a safe and clean space. Unfortunately, we have been put in this situation. We're trying to do the best we can. We've always done the best we can with what we've got."[9]

In Boston, Massachusetts, teenagers in the Roxbury Environmental Empowerment Project (REEP) have worked for environmental justice. Like other groups, REEP has conducted toxic tours, and every year the group takes hundreds of students on a tour of Dudley Square, a commercial center in Boston's Roxbury neighborhood. There, in 1998, REEP tackled air pollution by forming a coalition to investigate and learn whether emissions from diesel buses and trucks were responsible for the high rate of respiratory problems, particularly asthma, in Roxbury. Young people led a march demanding clean air and an air pollution monitoring system. During their demonstration, REEP handed out "tickets" (actually pamphlets) to educate drivers about air pollution from idling vehicles.

The group eventually convinced the city to retrofit its diesel buses to run on cleaner-burning fuel and to set up a system called AirBeat to monitor air quality. REEP teen member Stanley Wiggins notes, "I consider the air monitor to be our greatest accomplishment because it gives us concrete, visual evidence as to why Roxbury is overburdened by air pollution."[10]

Shameka Blake-Jackson, who worked with REEP for three years until she went to college in 2009, says,

Being at REEP allowed me to look at things differently. I've changed as a person. I'm in a whole different state of mind. I've learned more about my community. I learned that asthma doesn't have to be in your genes, it can come from air pollution, by trucks idling. I didn't know that an idling car pollutes. . . . I learned that in urban lower-income communities, asthma rates are higher than suburban communities.

For Blake-Jackson, who has suffered from asthma all her life, sharing what she has learned with younger students gives her the opportunity to help the "next generation."[11]

Toxic Dumping on Indian Lands

"We don't have the complexion for protection!" This slogan from a sign on Navajo land succinctly sums up what environmental racism is about. A number of investigative reports have shown that "Native American reservations have become prime targets of waste disposal firms. As of 1992, the leaders of more than 100 reservations have been approached by such firms," according to Deborah Robinson of the World Council of Churches. She adds,

Many waste-disposal companies have attempted to avoid state regulations (which are often tougher than federal regulations) by targeting Native lands.

Because of their quasi-independent status, Native American reservations are not covered by state environmental regulations. In 1991, a Connecticut-based company proposed to build a 6,000 acre municipal landfill on [South Dakota's Rosebud] Sioux land. . . . Local residents founded the Good Road Coalition and appealed to the Tribal Council to rescind the contract signed with the company. They were able to block construction of the landfill. [12]

Yet, because of extreme poverty on their reservations, some tribal elders in the west and east have agreed to allow toxic dump sites on their lands in exchange for financial payments, sometimes in the millions of dollars.

Besides the health hazards of toxic waste dumping, a disproportionate number of Native Americans suffer from exposure to radioactive contaminants. Consider the Navajo boys and men in the Navajo reservation that covers 26,000 square miles in the area where Utah, Arizona, New Mexico, and Colorado meet. The U.S. government recruited the poverty-stricken males in the late 1940s and early 1950s to work in uranium mines. While in their thirties and forties, many of the miners died of cancer or respiratory diseases caused by radioactive gas produced from the decay of radium in uranium ore. According to Chip Ward, author and founder of HEAL Utah, a grassroots group that has led the opposition to the disposal of nuclear waste in Utah, "from 1946 into the late 1970s, more than forty million tons of uranium ore was mined near Navajo communities. For three generations now, they have been breathing uranium-laden dust from mine tailings and drinking from wells tainted with minute traces of radioactive mining waste." Ward notes:

More than a thousand mines were abandoned on the reservation. For every 4 pounds of uranium extracted, 996 pounds of radioactive refuse was left behind in waste pits and piles swept by the wind and leached into local drinking water. In addition to the hundreds, perhaps thousands, of Navajo miners who sickened and died of cancer and respiratory illnesses—it's hard to say just how many, since nobody in power bothered to keep track—

Nuclear power plants like this one have tried to dispose of their radioactive waste on Native American lands.

epidemiological studies reveal a terrible ongoing toll. Navajo children living near the mines and mills suffered five times the rate of bone cancer and 15 times the rate of testicular and ovarian cancers as other Americans. Exposure to uranium has also been linked to kidney damage and birth defects.[13]

In 2005, the Navajo Nation banned uranium mining on all of their land, but Hydro Resources Inc. petitioned the U.S. Nuclear Regulatory Commission to take the land under a U.S. code that would simply reclassify the area as "not Indian

It Happened to Winona LaDuke

Since she was an eighteen-year-old student at Harvard University, Winona LaDuke has been working on Native American environmental campaigns all over the West. She is a legally recognized member of the Anishinaabeg (Ojibwe) White Earth tribe; when she was born, her father enrolled her in his tribe. Although she did not grow up on the White Earth reservation, she often visited there and took part in pow-wows and other ceremonies. After graduating from Harvard, she moved to the White Earth reservation and founded the White Earth Land Recovery Project (WELRP) in 1989. One of the project's purposes is to buy back land that once was part of the reservation. LaDuke also speaks on many occasions about the need to protect indigenous lands from toxic waste dumping, particularly nuclear waste. She also directs and operates several environmental organizations, and during the 1996 and 2000 presidential election campaigns, she was the Green Party's vice-presidential candidate running with Ralph Nader.

country." Despite the dangers of uranium mines and mills, the U.S. Nuclear Regulatory Commission granted a mining license to Hydro Resources Inc., which plans to develop claims near the Navajo communities of Church Rock and Crownpoint in New Mexico. The mines would threaten an aquifer that is a source of drinking water for the communities. As of May 2011, a Navajo group had petitioned the Inter-American Commission on Human Rights to stop the uranium mining project near the two villages. Whether the commission will take action is uncertain, but the Navajo hope that the international publicity will help their cause.

Dumping Toxic Trash in Poor Countries

Every year, the United States scraps 400 million units of electronic devices—used computers, televisions, cell phones, PDAs, and other gadgets. Electronic trash

See This Flick: *Toxic Soup*

The documentary film *Toxic Soup* (2010), released as a DVD in 2011, is by Rory Owen Delaney. It may not be easy to watch and listen to as people tell their stories about toxic emissions from manufacturing companies that endanger their health. Delaney interviewed people in eight different states to document their fights to prevent dangerous chemicals from polluting the air, water, and land in their communities. In many cases, the people trying to protect their health are like the biblical David who fights Goliath. While people suffer, corporate executives find ways to manipulate the political system to ignore or suppress environmental reforms.

---

also collects in such industrialized nations as Britain and Germany. Where do these throwaways go? Folks who want to live green try to take their electronic trash to a recycler. But some of these recyclers are illegally shipping electronics overseas to Asia and Africa where the trash is piled in heaps at dumps in poor communities and smashed to recover parts. Teenagers and younger children scavenge at the dumps and are exposed to poisonous chemicals, like mercury, lead, cadmium, polyvinyl chlorides, and other toxins that can cause brain damage, kidney disease, and cancer.

In 2010, a *60 Minutes* episode followed a shipment of cathode ray tubes (CRTs) from an Englewood, Colorado, recycler to Tacoma, Washington, and then to the small town of Guiyu in southern China. Shipping CRTs from the United States to another country is illegal. In Guiyu, investigative reporter Scott Pelley found a recycling center where

women were heating circuit boards over a coal fire, pulling out chips and pouring off the lead solder. Men were using what is literally a medieval acid recipe to extract gold. Pollution has ruined the town. Drinking water is trucked in. Scientists have studied the area and discovered that Guiyu has the highest levels of cancer-causing dioxins in the world. They found pregnancies are six times more likely to end in miscarriage, and that seven out of ten kids have too much lead in their blood.[14]

When the owner of the Colorado recycling company was confronted with evidence of the illegal shipment, he denied any knowledge of the container's content. But the U.S. Government Accountability Office confirmed what *60 Minutes* had found and also reported that more than forty other companies shipped toxic electronics overseas.

Such illegal operations also take place in Great Britain. According to an investigative report by the *Independent* newspaper in conjunction with the environmental organization Greenpeace, "hundreds of thousands of discarded items, which under British law must be dismantled or recycled by specialist contractors, are being packaged into cargo containers and shipped to countries such as Nigeria and Ghana, where they are stripped of their raw metals by young men and children working on poisoned waste dumps." Part of the evidence from their investigation was a broken television that had been equipped with a tracking device. The TV traveled from a dock in Essex, England, to Lagos, Nigeria, "where up to 15 shipping containers of discarded electronics from Europe and Asia arrive every day. At least a third of the contents of each container is broken beyond use and transferred to dumps where waste pickers scavenge amid a cocktail of burning heavy metals and dioxins."[15]

Environmental and social justice activists in England, the United States, and some European countries are campaigning for stronger laws to protect people who are victims of toxic dumping wherever it occurs. One promising effort in the United States is the Responsible Electronics Recycling Act of 2011. It has bipartisan sponsorship in both the U.S. House and Senate. The bill restricts the export of electronics containing certain toxic chemicals to developing countries. It would still allow exports of tested and working parts and products, as well as products or components under warranty, exported by the manufacturers for warranty repairs, and products subject to recalls. Sponsors hope the proposed law will encourage more recycling of electronics at home rather than abroad, where people are endangered because of toxic dumping.

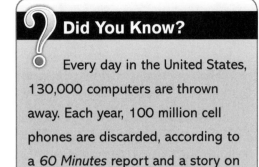

Did You Know?

Every day in the United States, 130,000 computers are thrown away. Each year, 100 million cell phones are discarded, according to a 60 *Minutes* report and a story on CBS *News.*[16]

Notes

1. "Toxic City: This Is Where I Live," *holamun2.com* (news special transcript), April 22, 2008, www.holamun2.com/shows/news-special/mun2-news-toxic-city (accessed May 28, 2011).

2. Bankole Thompson, "U.S. Youth on Frontlines of Green Justice Struggles," *ips.org*, June 24, 2010, www.ips.org/TV/wsf/us-youth-on-frontlines-of-green-justice-struggles (accessed August 20, 2011).

3. Bankole Thompson, "U.S. Youth on Frontlines of Green Justice Struggles," *ips.org*, June 24, 2010, www.ips.org/TV/wsf/us-youth-on-frontlines-of-green-justice-struggles (accessed May 28, 2011).

4. Chief Seattle, "Message to the Modern World," *Studies in Comparative Religion*, Summer 1976, www.studiesincomparativereligion.com/public/articles/Message_to_the_Modern_World-by_Chief_Seattle.aspx (accessed May 29, 2011).

5. Sierra Club, "Toxic Tours: Challenging Polluters' Business Sense(s)," *EJ Times*, January–March 2001, p. 3.

6. Robert D. Bullard, Paul Mohai, Robin Saha, and Beverly Wright, *Toxic Waste and Race at Twenty: 1987–2007* (Cleveland, OH: United Church of Christ Justice and Witness Ministries, March 2007), p. 146.

7. Vu-Bang Nguyen, "Youth Group Shuts Down Toxic Waste Facility," *urbanhabitat.org*, 2007, http://urbanhabitat.org/cj/v.nguyen (accessed May 30, 2011).

8. Kari Lydersen, "Fighting the Cloud Factory," *In These Times*, July 6, 2009, www.inthese-times.com/article/4519/fighting_the_cloud_factory (accessed May 30, 2011).

9. Christopher Weber, "Chicago Teens Discuss the Way They've Challenged School Pollution," *Emagazine*, January 1, 2011, www.emagazine.com/includes/print-article/magazine/8292 (accessed May 30, 2011).

10. Penn Loh, et al., "From Asthma to AirBeat: Community-Driven Monitoring of Fine Particulates and Black Carbon in Roxbury, Massachusetts," *Environmental Health Perspectives*, April 2002, p. 301, www.ncbi.nlm.nih.gov/pmc/articles/PMC1241176/pdf/ehp110s-000297.pdf (accessed May 31, 2011).

11. Shameka Blake-Jackson, *2009 REEP Report*, www.ace-ej.org/shamekas_story (accessed May 31, 2011).

12. Deborah M. Robinson, "Environmental Racism: Old Wine in a New Bottle," *Echoes Magazine*, 2007, www.wcc-coe.org/wcc/what/jpc/echoes/echoes-17-02.htm (accessed June 2, 2011).

13. Chip Ward, "Uranium Frenzy in the West," *Tomdispatch.com*, June 19, 2008, www.tomdispatch.com/post/174946/chip_ward_uranium_frenzy_in_the_west (accessed June 3, 2011).

14. CBS News, "Following the Trail of Toxic E-Waste," *CBSnews.com*, January 8, 2010 (first published November 9, 2008; updated August 27, 2009), www.cbsnews.com/2102-18560_162-4579229.html?tag=contentMain;contentBody (accessed July 9, 2011).

15. Cahal Milmo, "Dumped in Africa: Britain's Toxic Waste," *The Independent*, February 18, 2009, www.independent.co.uk/news/world/africa/dumped-in-africa-britain8217s-toxic-waste-1624869.html (accessed July 9, 2011).

16. CBS News, "Following the Trail of Toxic E-Waste," *60 Minutes*, January 8, 2010, www.cbsnews.com/stories/2008/11/06/60minutes/main4579229.shtml (accessed October 22, 2011).

PROTECTING WILDLIFE

"I hate the way the world is becoming—animals are treated so badly and pollution is so bad. I have always wanted to take action and have tried to help. The whaling issue is something good to start with because whaling is something that can hopefully be stopped."
—*Alexandra Weinstein of Essex, Massachusetts,*
a teenager who initiated a "Save the Whales" program[1]

"Parma [Ohio] Teens Honored for Saving Wildlife"

"Alaska Teens Fight to Save Wild Salmon"

"Teen Sells Bracelets to Raise Money for Oil Spill Cleanup"

"Teen Turtle Defender"

"Student Fundraiser Helps Save Wildlife"

"Teen Sacrifices College Fund to Help Save Florida Wildlife from Oil"

"Teens Helping Save Manatees from Extinction"

These newspaper headlines only hint at the stories about youth who help protect wildlife. In some cases, their actions involve simple but important projects, such as the Parma, Ohio, teens who collected dishwashing soap to clean birds and other animals covered in oil from the 2010 disastrous BP oil spill in the Gulf of Mexico. The teen turtle defender is Chris, who had read that the population of diamondback terrapins was declining in Maryland's Chesapeake Bay because of overharvesting for turtle soup enjoyed in Asia. The teenager and his father gathered petitions to save the turtles and presented them to the Maryland legislature, which eventually passed a law to ban terrapin harvesting.

In 2010, a group of teenagers in Cameron Parish, Louisiana, were part of a three-day "Marsh Maneuvers" effort to plant marsh grasses along the coast. One of the group notes, "Once this grass takes over the sand will get caught and it will build up this big dune. . . . This will stop the ocean action so basically we're building a levee and it's a natural levee because the wind builds it. I'm excited because that means our homes aren't going to get eaten in fifty years, so there'll still be a Cameron Parish."[2]

Amanda Bozorgi, who was a year-long participant in the Lake Forest (Illinois) Open Lands Association's Center for Conservation Leadership (CCL) explains,

> I was involved in a community service project WOLVES (Working Open Lands Volunteers Environmental Students) in my school. I had to organize workdays throughout the year. There were 10 workdays, which ranged from cleaning up the beach on National Beach Cleanup Day to pulling garlic mustard at Mellody Farm Nature Preserve. We usually met the first Saturday of the month and averaged eight to 10 volunteers. Sometimes there were as many as 20. Sometimes there were only two. It depended on the day.[3]

In Hopkinton, Massachusetts, high school students enter an annual Environthon, a state competition on environmental science. The Envirothon includes topics on wildlife, from aquatic life to habitat protection. Student teams select an environmental subject and prepare a presentation on how their community is involved with the topic. Student Gwen Burnham-Fay reports,

> The Environthon is a way for everyone in the state who cares about the environment to come together and do something positive. . . . By educating ourselves about a new topic every year, each team and school is able to broaden their knowledge of the environment and how we can help it. I think it's an awesome way to put everything we preach into action, especially the project/presentation section of it. . . . It's fun to compete with people who share the same interests and want the same things for the

earth that you do. Overall, it's just an awesome experience that really can diversify how we interact with our environment.[4]

In 2009, seventeen-year-old Alex Heeb of Missouri began his mission to stop box turtle races, which are held at festivals and other events across the United States. Why go after these popular attractions? Alex explains,

Several years ago I developed an interest in turtles, and I befriended a wild turtle I named Minn. Minn lived in a dry creek bed where I found her frequently, and she never turned down the treats I offered. I decided to enter her in a turtle race at a local festival. Although I had participated before, this was the first time I had used my own turtle. During the race, Minn refused all the treats I offered her, and she seemed to be upset. I released Minn in the exact spot where I found her, but I felt bad for what I put her through. I still find her occasionally to this day.

After his experience with Minn, Alex conducted extensive research on box turtle races in about three dozen states and found that the turtles are "frequently dehydrated, underfed and sometimes have injuries." And if they are released back into their habitat, many cannot adapt well and some develop pneumonia. Others carry diseases that infect turtles in the wild. Alex told *Humane Teen*, part of the Humane Society, that he plans to continue his efforts to try to stop turtle racing: "I hope to get a degree in wildlife ecology so I can continue to work with wildlife and turtles. If I get the chance, I would also like to work with endangered box turtles that live in Mexico."[5]

Saving wild salmon is a project of the Alaska Youth for Environmental Action (AYEA). The Renewable Resources Coalition writes,

Many of the teens in AYEA are from rural communities that rely on salmon for survival. But it's more than just the environmental and economic significance; salmon is also culturally important to them. Wild salmon populations have been declining across western North America for decades, and for many Alaskans, that loss puts their cultural and spiritual way of life in danger.[6]

AYEA went to the state capital in 2011 to deliver petitions to legislators about the importance of wild salmon. Also they are raising awareness of how a proposed gold and copper mine at Bristol Bay would generate billions of tons of waste, contaminating land and water and destroying salmon habitat and fisheries.

Protecting manatees—those gentle mammals that often congregate in the warm waters like those off Florida shores in winter months—is what Save the Manatee Club is all about. Youth and adults donate funds through the club's Adopt-a-Manatee program that helps protect manatees. They often are wounded or killed by propellers of boats speeding through their habitat. Another group, Kids Making a Difference (KMAD), does its part in manatee protection. The nonprofit organization was founded by Stephanie Cohen when she was just an elementary student and read about an injured baby manatee. As a teenager, Stephanie self-published her book *Sydney Saves a Species: Message from the Manatee* through KMAD. She explains that the book is based on her own experience and is the "story of Sydney, an ordinary young girl who does the extraordinary to help a baby manatee. . . . All proceeds benefit injured and endangered marine mammals."[7]

Protecting Feathered Wildlife

High school sophomore Mac Murphy, along with Amanda Bozorgi, was one of the seventeen teenagers from Lake County, Illinois, who spent a year involved in Lake Forest Open Lands Association's Center for Conservation Leadership program, which includes monthly workshops and personal stewardship projects. Murphy reports, "I built 13 wood duck nesting boxes. I put eight in Lake County

Bald Eagles Rule from Their Roost

The city of Pinellas Park, Florida, was ready to raze an old structure near its Freedom Lake and build a recreation center for young people in its place. But the plans did not materialize after park officials discovered two bald eagles nesting on a nearby cell tower. The eagles had first rights to occupation. Bald eagles, the national bird, were once in danger of becoming extinct but were removed from the endangered species list in 2007. However, nesting bald eagles are protected under state law and by the federal Bald and Golden Eagle Protection Act (Eagle Act) and the Migratory Bird Treaty Act. According to the Eagle Act, anyone who interferes with eagles' normal breeding, feeding, or sheltering behavior can be fined and jailed. In Pinellas Park, city officials and the Florida Fish and Wildlife Conservation Commission conferred and decided that if demolition and construction went ahead, the eagles in their roost atop the tower would be disturbed during their breeding season from October to May. Even after that, the eagles might not leave. Or they might take flight but return the next year. According to the Fish and Wildlife Conservation Commission, a nest must be vacant for five years to be considered abandoned. Thus, the city made plans to build elsewhere, and the bald eagles remained in charge—from their roost.[8]

Forest Preserve District lands and four on private property. When the wood duck population started to decline, hunters, such as myself, started reducing the hunting season, which helps [ducks] to come back."[9]

When she was a senior in high school, Gabriela McCall Delgado of Puerto Rico was concerned about the diminishing bird population in her neighborhood, so she began photographing birds and their habitat. She was able to determine that the decrease in the number of birds was related to the increase in building projects, which were destroying nesting and food sources for birds. With her photographs, which she has shown to groups in Puerto Rico and the United States, she has raised awareness of the need to protect natural habitats for birds.

In Ithaca, New York, teenagers who are part of the Youth Horticulture Apprentice Program (YHAP) spent several days during the 2009 summer season to install a bird habitat garden, which was part of Ithaca's Children's Garden, a place to bring young people and nature together. Because deer live in a nearby area and like feeding on garden plants, the teens fenced the habitat garden as well as put more than one hundred flowering and other green plants in the ground to attract birds. In addition, they constructed a child-size bird nest using an old wicker Papasan chair frame as a base and weaving wild grapevines within it as birds would do. The nest was lined with straw, forming a comfortable place for a child to relax. Spenser Blinn, one of the teenagers involved, says, "The bird nest was very successful as was the bird garden. It was great fun and hard work." Uriel Walker agrees: "The bird garden installation was a good example of teamwork. The nest building was also a good example of teamwork and I think kids will like it a lot. It was also a good example of reuse. It came together better than I thought and looks just like a nest."[10]

Backyard Help for Wildlife

If you have a backyard, you can take action to protect wildlife. Planting a tree is one way to provide homes for a variety of wild creatures, from birds to raccoons to tree frogs. Evergreen species provide year-round cover and shelter, and fruit- or nut-bearing plants provide a food source. You can allow a part of the backyard to grow "wild"—letting tall grasses and weeds become hiding places for animals.

If you want to attract birds, put a bird house or bird feeder in your yard. If your home has large windows or sliding glass doors, place cutouts or hanging objects that will prevent birds from flying into the glass and injuring themselves. The U.S. Fish and Wildlife Service has an Office of Migratory Bird Management that works with groups and individuals to conserve and manage migratory birds. The agency offers information about backyard habitats for birds and wildlife.

You might want to attract bats to your backyard to control insects. You probably have heard the scary stories about bats—the flying mammals are thought to be a danger to people. But contrary to popular beliefs, bats are *not* blind, they will *not* get into your hair, and they are *not* like vampires that suck blood from your neck. You may not want bats in your home, but they are natural pest removers. Bats have a sensitive sonar, or sound wave, system that helps them detect insects and determine whether they are edible. The most common bat species in the United States can devour five hundred mosquitoes an hour. Within twenty-four to thirty-six hours, a bat will eat enough insects, including moths and beetles, to equal its own body weight. They also pollinate plants, and by eating fruit, they scatter seeds into the soil.

Bat Conservation International (BCI) is an organization that disseminates information about bats worldwide and campaigns to protect some species from extinction. To protect these wildlife animals, you can build or buy a bat house. BCI's website (www.batcon.org) provides instructions for building bat houses or lists of vendors who sell BCI-certified bat houses.

It is possible to create a garden that attracts wildlife, whether you place it on a balcony of an apartment, on a large farm, in a vacant lot, or elsewhere. If you provide food, water, cover, and a place for wildlife to raise their young, the National Wildlife Federation could declare your garden an official "Certified Wildlife Habitat." There are 140,000 certified sites across the United States. Instructions for how to begin the process of certification are on the federation's website.[11]

Wild in the Neighborhood

If you are familiar with wildlife outside your home, you probably are aware also of wildlife in your neighborhood or town—pigeons, a variety of song birds, snakes, turtles, raccoons, wild turkeys, deer, and even coyotes in some rural and suburban areas and alligators in southern states, to name some examples. With increasing urban sprawl in many U.S. areas, people are encroaching on the habitats of wild creatures. Some of these animals, reptiles, and birds can be pesky or a danger to small pets and people—alligators, for example. So how do people and pets stay safe and still protect wildlife?

Teenagers in Florida thought they had the answer. When their school bus stopped in a Pasco County area to let off a student, four boys spotted an alligator, jumped off their bus, "then chased, wrestled and captured [it] in a rural pasture." They taped closed the jaws of the four-foot alligator, according to a news report, and in spite of the bus driver's protests, the boys declared they would not get back on the bus without the reptile. The boys took the alligator to one of their homes, depositing it in a parent's truck. Although the alligator was released back into the wild near the Withlacoochee River, the boys were reprimanded, and the bus driver was suspended from her job with pay. A school official says, "In 36 years of education, I've never come across an alligator on a bus."[12]

In some states, dealing with wildlife can be brutal, especially if there are killing contests. Usually these contests are advertised as population or nuisance control, but they are simply an excuse for wanton animal slaughter, say wildlife advocates, conservation officials, and hunters who believe the events are unethical and turn hunting into a cash-fueled spectacle. In some cases, the contests are called "thrill-killing." In 2011, for example, the Wisconsin Department of Natural Resources "uncovered a ring of 12 young men between the ages of 16 and 19 who held contests over two years to see how many wild animals they could kill. The contests involved beating to death raccoons and running down deer with cars."[13]

In Arizona, participants in such contests compete for prizes to see who can kill the most animals. According to the Humane Society, "In a party-like atmosphere, contestants sometimes kill hundreds of coyotes and foxes just for fun and money." In Idaho, wolf hunts are conducted for prizes. Prairie dogs are the targets for contests in Colorado, where contestants compete for body counts but also "may bet extra points for 'specialty' shots. These include the 'acrobat,'

It Happened to Alexis Ulrich

Photographs and stories about Canada's annual seal hunt upset Alexis Ulrich of Lakewood, Colorado, so much that she had to take action. As a college student, she boycotts any seafood products from Canada and speaks out regularly about the brutal practice of shooting, stabbing, or bludgeoning baby seals to death. The slaughtered seals are skinned for their pelts. Ulrich puts information about seal hunts on her Facebook page, makes class presentations about the practice, and writes letters to newspapers urging the Canadian government to stop seal hunts. As of 2011 that had not happened, but Ulrich continues her protests, as do many others who want the hunts banned.

Ulrich also is passionate about protecting pets like cats and dogs from abuse. She began an Animal Rights Club at the University of Colorado, Denver, where she is enrolled. The club's mission is to raise awareness of the need for animal protection, seek funds for animal welfare, and campaign for laws to protect animals. Her efforts on behalf of all kinds of animals brought her a 2010 Humane Teen of the Year award.

in which the impact of the bullet flips the animal into the air; the 'chamois shot,' in which the bullet literally explodes the animal, sending a large piece of pelt flying through the air; and the 'red mist,' in which the victim is obscured in a spray of blood."[14]

The humane way to rid a neighborhood of wild animals, say their defenders, is to tranquilize them and then remove them. But every state has its own set of regulations for managing wildlife. Some allow the use of cages to capture wild animals, especially small critters, which then may be relocated or killed. Regulated hunting to "harvest" or control an overabundant population of animals is another method of wildlife management. Deer populations, for example, have increased dramatically in heavily forested or wooded areas of some states, and as cities and

What Would You Do?

Technically, farm animals (like cows and chickens) are considered domesticated and not "wild" animals, but the life of one feathered creature—a baby chick—was saved from death by teenager Whitney Hillman of Concordia, Kansas. In 2010, Whitney was taking a science class at Concordia High School, and as part of an assignment, each student was supposed to select a baby chick from a brood, name it, and keep it in a cage with other broiler chickens until time to kill and package it for consumption. Whitney named her chick Chicklett and repeatedly told her teacher she objected to the project and could not kill her chick. She agonized over the fact that she was required to slaughter it. She says, "On the day of the scheduled slaughter, I knew I couldn't go through with killing my chicken. I went into the school with a plan and a big purse. . . . I walked into the class minutes before the slaughter was to occur and rescued my Chicklett."[15] She ran out of school and took her chicken home, which is licensed as an animal foster home to save animals from euthanasia at a local shelter. As a result of her action, Whitney received in-school suspension for two days, and many students in the science class ridiculed her. Still Whitney felt she had done the right thing and intends to continue to voice her objections to such science projects.

Whitney's mother was asked how she felt about the science class and slaughtering the chickens, and she says, "I think it is barbaric. I think teens are unskilled in this and to hand 40 children knives and a live animal in class is a senseless cruelty. The animals suffered and I feel confident that the children did too."[16] On the other hand, school officials support the science project. In the principal's words, "We come from an agricultural part of the nation, and our students need to understand that food doesn't magically appear on our plates at home or in a restaurant. Animals are used to feed us, and there is a process in the raising of those animals, from birth to consumption. These students learned that process in this Animal Science class, taught by a dedicated and caring teacher."[17]

What would you do if you were expected to slaughter a chicken in a school class? Do you think Whitney did the right thing?

See This Flick: *Play Again*

The award-winning film *Play Again* is a 2010 documentary that follows six teenagers who, like most young people, spend five to fifteen hours a day using electronic media rather than being outdoors and involved in nature. This eighty-minute documentary asks "Is our connection to nature disappearing down the digital rabbit hole?" *Play Again* explores the changing balance between the virtual and natural worlds and takes the teens into the wilderness, where there is no electricity, cell phone coverage, or electronic media. As the young people explore, they discover a stream with water bubbling over rocks, balance themselves while walking on fallen logs, make a bow and arrow, and generally connect with the wilderness. Robin Mann, president of the Sierra Club, writes, "It is a powerful film, revealing that we are allowing our young people to be so profoundly disconnected from the natural world and denying them the opportunity to fully develop their senses. We can and must . . . give [young people] the access to the natural world that is so essential to their development."[18]

---

suburbs expand, the deer's natural food supply diminishes and they forage for food in ornamental gardens and on croplands. Deer also can be a danger to themselves and humans as they cross roadways and collide with vehicles.

In some cases, conflicts with wild animals can be reduced if garbage containers are covered and secured. An Alaska resident can be fined for not having bear-proof cans or dumpsters or for leaving trash containers open—an invitation for bears or other animals to feed.

Nonlethal methods to manage wildlife are studied, discussed, and implemented in many states. Just a quick browse of the term *non-lethal wildlife management* on the Internet generates tens of thousands of sites with hundreds of suggestions for repelling wild creatures, ranging from pigeons to bears and rodents to wolves.

Wildlife Preservation Organizations

Numerous local, state, national, and global organizations work to preserve wildlife. Many are organizations that strive to protect one type of animal, such as Save the Manatee or Save the Polar Bear clubs, and they usually ask for donations to support their efforts. Others are broader in scope, focusing on all types of wildlife conservation. They have websites where they solicit funds and describe their missions. Here are a few examples:

- The World Wildlife Fund (WWF) says it's the "leading conservation organization." It "works in 100 countries and is supported by 1.2 million members in the United States and close to 5 million globally. WWF's unique way of working combines global reach with a foundation in science, involves action at every level from local to global, and ensures the delivery of innovative solutions that meet the needs of both people and nature."[19]

- The National Wildlife Federation (NWF) "works to inspire Americans to protect wildlife for our children's future. As the nation's largest conservation organization, NWF and its 4 million supporters are committed to sustaining the nature of America for the benefit of people and wildlife."[20]

- Defenders of Wildlife is "one of the country's leaders in science-based, results-oriented wildlife conservation." It is committed "to saving imperiled wildlife and championing the Endangered Species Act, the landmark law that protects them."[21]

- The Natural Resources Defense Council (NRDC) is a nonprofit environmental organization that uses "law, science and the support of 1.3 million members and online activists to protect the planet's wildlife and wild places and to ensure a safe and healthy environment for all living things."[22]

- The U.S. Fish and Wildlife Service works "to conserve, protect and enhance fish, wildlife, and plants and their habitats for the continuing benefit of the American people."[23]

- The Nature Conservancy works "around the world to protect ecologically important lands and waters for nature and people."[24]
- Wildlife in Crisis cares for "injured and orphaned wildlife." The organization has "received an average of 10,000 calls about wildlife every year."[25]

Notes

1. The Humane Society of the United States, "Alexandra Weinstein," *Humane Teen*, n.d. www.humaneteen.org/?q=node/265 (accessed June 5, 2011).
2. Theresa Schmidt, "Teens Planting Marsh Grass to Save Wetlands," *KPLC 7 News*, June 8, 2010, www.kplctv.com/story/12614341/teens-planting-marsh-grass-to-save-wetlands?redirected=true (accessed June 8, 2011).
3. Linda Blaser, "Teens Graduate from LFOLA Program," *Lake Forester*, May 12, 2011, http://lakeforest.suntimes.com/5183684-417/teens-graduate-from-lfola-program.html (accessed June 3, 2011).
4. Helen Prunty Krispien, "Teens Accept Task of Protecting Environment," *Hopkinton Crier*, June 18, 2010, www.wickedlocal.com/hopkinton/news/education/x1808626197/Teens-accept-task-of-protecting-environment#axzz1NwDxRBrt (accessed June 4, 2011).
5. The Humane Society of the United States, "Alex Heeb," *Humane Teen*, n.d., www.humane-teen.org/?q=node/762 (accessed June 5, 2011).
6. "Alaska Teens Fight to Save Wild Salmon," *Renewable Resources Coalition*, February 3, 2011, www.renewableresourcescoalition.org/newsroom/2011-02-03/alaska-teens-fight-to-save-wild-salmon (accessed July 10, 2011).
7. "Stephanie Cohen," *The Humane Society of the United States*, January 28, 2011, www.humanesociety.org/about/departments/students/student_voices/advisory_board/stephanie_cohen.html (accessed July 11, 2011).
8. Anne Lindberg, "Bald Eagle Nest Derails Pinellas Park Rec Center Renovation," *St. Petersburg Times*, October 22, 2010, www.tampabay.com/news/localgovernment/article1123004.ece (accessed June 9, 2011).
9. Linda Blaser, "Teens Graduate from LFOLA Program," *Lake Forester*, May 12, 2011, http://lakeforest.suntimes.com/5183684-417/teens-graduate-from-lfola-program.html (accessed June 3, 2011).
10. Cornell Laboratory of Ornithology, "Ithaca Children's Garden," *Cornell University Cooperative Extension*, n.d., www.birds.cornell.edu/celebration/community/Spotlight/Partners/ithaca-children-s-garden-planting-a-bird-friendly-garden#portlet-navigation-tree (accessed June 9, 2011).
11. "Find Volunteer Opportunities," *National Wildlife Federation*, 2011, www.nwf.org/Volunteer/Find-Opportunities.aspx (accessed October 23, 2011).
12. Rebecca Catalanello, "Bus Driver: Students Refused to Leave Gator," *St. Petersburg Times*,

March 10, 2003, www.sptimes.com/2004/03/10/news_pf/Tampabay/Bus_driver__Students_ .shtml (accessed June 5, 2011).

13. Ron Seely, "Conservation Wardens Uncover Wildlife Thrill-Killing Ring," *Wisconsin State Journal*, February 9, 2011, http://host.madison.com/wsj/news/local/environment/ article_4b1494dc-3491-11e0-91f8-001cc4c002e0.html (accessed June 6, 2011).

14. The Humane Society of the United States, "Sample Letter to the Editor," *Stop Wildlife Killing Contests*, n.d., www.humanesociety.org/assets/pdfs/hunting/PrairieDogSteppedLtrs.pdf (accessed June 5, 2011).

15. The Humane Society of the United States, "Whitney Hillman," *Humane Teen*, 2010, www .humaneteen.org/?q=node/1350 (accessed June 9, 2011).

16. The Humane Society of the United States, "Whitney Hillman," *Humane Teen*, 2010, www .humaneteen.org/?q=node/1350 (accessed June 9, 2011).

17. Michael Strand, "Not Chicklett!" *Salina Journal*, October 20, 2010, www.salina.com/News/ Story/chicklett (accessed June 9, 2011).

18. *Play Again* Reviews, n.d., http://playagainfilm.com/press/reviews/ (accessed November 8, 2011).

19. "Who We Are: About WWF," *World Wildlife Fund*, 2011, www.worldwildlife.org/who/index .html (accessed July 10, 2011).

20. "Our Work Protecting Wildlife and Habitat," *National Wildlife Federation*, 2011, www.nwf .org/wildlife/what-we-do.aspx (accessed July 10, 2011).

21. "About Us," *Defenders of Wildlife*, 2011, www.defenders.org/about_us/index.php?utm_ source=B_Version_NoFlash&utm_medium=Top_Nav&utm_content=AU&utm_ campaign=HP_AB_Round2 (accessed July 10, 2011).

22. "About NRDC: Who We Are," *Natural Resources Defense Council*, n.d., www.nrdc.org/about/ who_we_are.asp (accessed July 10, 2011).

23. "USFWS Mission Statement," *U.S. Fish and Wildlife Service*, n.d., www.fws.gov/mission .html (accessed July 10, 2011).

24. "About Us: Learn More about the Nature Conservancy," *The Nature Conservancy*, 2011, www .nature.org/aboutus/index.htm?s_intc=header (accessed July 10, 2011).

25. "About Us," *Wildlife in Crisis, Inc.*, n.d., www.wildlifeincrisis.com/about/index.htm (accessed July 10, 2011).

SAVING WATER RESOURCES

....

"It was astonishing how much trash we found. . . .
The cleanup put a lot of things in perspective for me."
—Paige Farrar, high school freshman, after taking part in a Florida shoreline cleanup[1]

Our earth sometimes has been called a water planet because its surface is more than 70 percent water. An estimated 97 percent of the total world supply of water is in the oceans, which contain dissolved mineral salts that have washed from the land and have accumulated over millions of years. Although organisms (including humans) need salt for life, the high salinity of seawater makes it unsuitable for drinking and agriculture. The human body and most crops need freshwater—that is, water with low concentrations of salt.

Throughout human history, people have fought and sometimes died for the right to a specific supply of freshwater. Humans, wildlife, domestic animals, and food crops depend on water resources for survival. In fact, writes Charles Fishman, author of *The Big Thirst*, "We used to build monuments—even temples—to water. The aqueducts of the Roman Empire are marvels of engineering and soaringly elegant design. . . . Today, water has drifted so far from civic celebration that many people visit the Roman aqueducts without any sense that they moved water, or how."[2]

Water Resources

To many people the term *water resources* prompts an image of what comes out of the faucet or an image of a river or lake for recreational activities. But there is a

What Is an Aquifer?

An aquifer is an important water resource, but contrary to popular belief, it is not an underground river, lake, or pool. Water in an aquifer is stored in porous rocks, like sandstone, or in rock fractures and in the tiny spaces, called pores, between soil particles. A layer of impermeable rock—solid rock that does not allow the water to seep through—usually lies beneath an aquifer or surrounds it. The water in the aquifer is replenished by rain, snow, and other precipitation. People usually have to dig wells to tap the water in aquifers, although some water from aquifers seeps into springs.

basic resource known as a watershed, an area of land that drains all the streams and rainfall to a common outlet, such as the outflow of a reservoir, mouth of a bay, or any point along a stream channel. In the United States, including Hawaii, Alaska, and Puerto Rico, there are 2,267 watersheds.[3]

The sizes and shapes of watersheds vary. For example, the Ohio River watershed is more than 154,000 square miles, begins in Pennsylvania, and drains into the Mississippi River, which flows to the Gulf of Mexico. The Mississippi River Watershed is the fourth largest in the world, "extending from the Allegheny Mountains in the east to the Rocky Mountains in the west. The watershed includes all or parts of 31 states and 2 Canadian provinces; it measures approximately 1.2 million square miles, covering about 40 percent of the lower 48 states."[4]

Because we all live in a watershed, everyone has a stake in keeping the water that drains from it protected from pollutants and overuse. Over decades, aquifers, rivers, streams, creeks, wetlands, lakes, and oceans have become contaminated with myriad pollutants from manufacturing plants, mining, agriculture, oil drilling, transportation, toxic dumping, deforestation, and other human activities. Storm water runoffs, leaking septic tanks, and waste water discharges also contaminate water. Polluted water endangers aquatic life, wildlife on land, and human health. Obviously protecting water resources and conserving water are important components of living green.

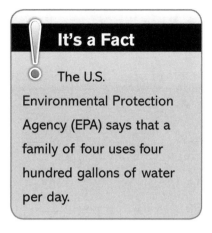

It's a Fact

The U.S. Environmental Protection Agency (EPA) says that a family of four uses four hundred gallons of water per day.

Ways to conserve water are posted on literally thousands of websites. Some of the most common advice is to turn off the tap whenever water is not needed; fix leaking faucets and toilets; take a short shower rather than a bath; wash a car or bike with a bucket of water and sponge rather than a hose; and sprinkle a garden or lawn in the evening or early morning to prevent the water from evaporating quickly.

Teenage twins Todd and Alex Davis in Santa Clarita Valley, California, set out in 2010 to convince a major water user, the Magic Mountain Theme Park, to conserve. The twins developed conservation suggestions for the park, including draining a lake to save one million gallons of water each year and planting indigenous plants that require low water input. They also worked with the park's staff to develop educational materials about water conservation.[5]

Saving Local Waterways

In the United States, news stories about water pollution were common in the 1950s and 1960s, and federal laws were passed in the 1970s to protect water supplies. The following are some examples: The Clean Water Act (CWA) of 1972 set standards for water quality and prohibited the flow of industrial wastes and municipal sewage into waterways. In 1974, the U.S. Safe Drinking Water Act gave the EPA authority to set limits for any contaminants in drinking water that would be a threat to public health. The Soil and Water Conservation Act of 1977 was passed to reduce soil erosion and agricultural sources of water pollutants. Other laws are in effect to protect ocean waters and marine mammals, such as porpoises, seals, manatees, whales, and dolphins.

Regardless of the laws, enforcement usually is weak, and individuals and groups across the United States have initiated projects and long-term programs to clean up and protect their local water sources. These may be aquifers, creeks, rivers, sloughs (slews), wetlands, lakes, or ocean coastal waters.

Testing water quality is a common activity for many students across the country. In a widespread testing of the Rio Grande River, students from the Santa Fe Indian School and about sixty other youth groups collected water samples in 2010 at various points along the river, which stretches nearly two thousand miles. One student, Irvin Pino, explains he was "testing for turbidity to see how cloudy the water is due to [soil] erosion. . . . I placed a stick on the bottom of a bucket and used a 'scale' to measure turbidity. If we barely see the stick on the bottom, it tells us there's a lot of erosion." Other students tested for iron and copper, coliform bacteria or other harmful organisms, and chemical components.[6]

The Bronx River in New York City is another waterway under inspection. It runs through an industrial section of the South Bronx, and the property along the river is owned by transportation and waste companies. However, a local nonprofit group called Rocking the Boat is helping teenagers study the river's ecology as well as learn boatbuilding and other job skills. Students in the program also collect water samples in the Bronx River, and if they suspect a pollutant, they report it to the park department or an environmental agency. According to a news report by Jenny Shalant,

The charts kept by the Bronx teens at Rocking the Boat show evidence of waste from the cement factories and sewage treatment plants that line the riverbanks. But as the students are discovering, refuse also flows into the river from street grates far across town. As in nearly 800 other municipalities across the country, New York City's rainwater runoff, household sewage, and industrial wastewater all run through the same pipes. And in a city as dense as New York, it only takes a tenth of an inch of rainfall for these pipes to back up and spew their grimy load directly into local waterways.[7]

On Rocking the Boat's website, some students reflect on their experiences both in their boatbuilding shop and on the water. Seventeen-year-old Rafael Salazar notes,

On my first day at Rocking the Boat, I remember that feeling of being in a new environment. My first thought was that boatbuilding was a task I wouldn't be able to accomplish. But I've learned new ways of looking at things since then. I've learned I'm good at working in a group and how to use new tools with skill. I like getting the job done and the feeling of accomplishment after.

Teenager Kristyl Colon declares, "Being a part of Rocking the Boat has definitely changed what I want out of life. It has made me realize my deep passion for environmental science and I have decided to major in Ecology for college." And Stephanie Cabral, age 20, recalls that her first day was exciting:

The people make the experience wonderful. It has allowed me to communicate with different people and I have more confidence. I've discovered that I'm a people person and now I want to pursue a degree in the social sciences. Rocking the Boat has made me realize that I can do what I set my mind to. My favorite memory is the time we spent on the Connecticut River. It was a week-long trip full of fun and bonding with friends.[8]

Another type of local waterway project is carried out by students at the Woodrow Wilson School in Bayonne, New Jersey. Once a month they monitor their "oyster garden." The students are reintroducing oysters to area waterways, not to increase a food source—the oysters are *not* safe to eat—but to keep the water clean. The mollusks help clean the water by feeding on suspended sediments (pollutants) and algae, filtering up to fifty gallons of water per day and enhancing conditions for the growth of underwater grasses that support other marine life.

In 2009, Sea Scouts of Bay Village, Ohio, came up with an invention to help remove trash from around a marina. Called a Flotsam Scoop, it consists of a sturdy aluminum handle with a half-bucket of mesh at the end, and the whole device weighs only five pounds. One of the scouts, university freshman Ethan Brewer, tells CNN, "We thought it'd be a good idea to invent something that we could actually give to the marinas to help them clean up these areas and help them keep up a good appearance."[9]

An Indianapolis, Indiana, project called the Great Indy Butt Out took place in 2009 when high school students from an environmental class cleaned up cigarette litter along a creek and the walkways to their school. A total of 41.4 pounds of litter was collected, which computed to about 110,414 butts and more than 30,000 milligrams of toxic nicotine removed from the environment.[10]

In 2010, one enterprising group of students in Manhattan, Kansas, constructed rain barrels, hoping to sell them to local residents and persuade them to collect rainwater for garden and lawn irrigation.

Across the nation in Elk Grove, California, a local waterway project in April 2011 cleaned up seven Elk Grove Creek sites that were mired in trash. Several high school students among the 770 volunteers found a shopping cart and filled it with so much trash they declared they had an "armored cart" full of throwaways. Other volunteers found such objects as "tires, basketballs, Styrofoam packaging, water bottles, a graffiti-covered mattress, and a kiddie swimming pool."[11]

Protecting Wetlands

Call it a slew, swamp, marsh, pond, mire, bog, bottomland, slough, or wet meadow—all are terms used to describe wetlands. Frequently wetlands have been depicted as frightening places or, at best, areas infested with mosquitoes, snakes, alligators, and other "unpleasant" creatures. Wetlands once were considered useless except when they could be mined for peat (a source of fuel) or stripped of trees. Thus it is not surprising that wetlands have been drained for farming or filled in and paved over for building projects. However, U.S. wetlands now are being identified and recognized as important water resources and vital links between land and water—ecosystems that need protection.

Wherever they are, wetlands are well worth protecting. Trappers and hunters long have appreciated the wildlife found in wetlands—ducks, geese, deer, mink, muskrat, and many types of fish and crustaceans. Wetlands act like sponges; they are filters, taking in waste products from surface runoffs before the water reaches a stream, river, lake, or estuary. They also filter out nitrogen and phosphorous, which could create eutrophication—that is, the nutrients enrich a body of water so that it fills with aquatic plants and is low in oxygen. As a result, fish and other aquatic life die. Another asset is flood control. Trees, shrubs, and other plants in wetlands can store overflow from streams, rivers, and lakes and prevent flooding of farmland and urban areas. Wetlands also recharge aquifers, which provide fresh water for human use.

In the United States, most wetlands are categorized as coastal (seawater) or inland (freshwater). Some are large, complex ecosystems, such as the Florida Everglades. Other wetlands are along small, spring-fed ponds or are riparian marshes along rivers and streams. There are wooded swamps called bottomland hardwood forests in southern states along flood plains or river valleys, particularly the Mississippi River.

One student group in Chesterland, Ohio, has received national attention for its efforts to inform their community about the value of wetlands. Students were alarmed when they learned that 90 percent of Ohio's wetlands had been destroyed over the past two hundred years. They formed the Wetlands Education Team (WET) to first teach other students about wetlands and then spread the message to their parents and their community. Clay M., one of the student founders of WET, writes,

We began more serious efforts when we joined the Ohio Division of Natural Resources to help bring back a very important bird species, the osprey. Ospreys are majestic birds of prey that feed on fish and nest in wetlands.

When the WET initiative began, osprey were classified as endangered in Ohio. With help from our county park district, we applied for and received several grants to build osprey nesting platforms in two counties. Since their installation, the platforms have been used by several nesting pairs, and the osprey's designation has been downgraded from endangered to threatened. [12]

During their spring break in 2011, Royal Oak High School students in Oakland County, California, traveled with chaperones to New Orleans to help plant 6,500 saplings in a cypress marsh that was destroyed by Hurricane Katrina in 2005. With the marsh restored, the threat of future flooding could be diminished. In addition, marshland could again become habitat for wildlife, from birds to fish and shellfish.

In Lee County, Florida, junior and senior high school students have been able to save a slough, a wetland ecosystem that is home for alligators, turtles, wading birds, and other animals. The students in an environmental education class known as the "Monday Group" began their project decades ago—in 1976—and as it has continued through the years, other students have taken the places of those who have left. Their efforts included an official plan to save the slough and a public education campaign, which convinced voters to raise their own taxes to preserve the area. The Monday Group's efforts helped create the Six Mile Cypress Slough Preserve, which currently consists of more than 2,500 acres.

However, there have been challenges through the years to protect the Six-Mile Cypress watershed from pollutants and draining of water resources by developers. To gain public support, Lee County Parks and Recreation opened a boardwalk in 1991 that allows visitors to observe the natural habitat and also learn how wetlands provide priceless but often hidden benefits, such as water purification and storage and natural flood control.

The Monday Group students continue their efforts, selecting a new project to tackle each year, such as campaigning for an ordinance to protect bald eagle habitats and efforts to save the manatees. You can connect with the group on Facebook and Myspace.

Cleaning Up Rivers, Bays, and Shorelines

Unimaginable! At least that is what people would think if they had never participated in a river, bay, or shoreline cleanup. Thousands of tires, hundreds of car parts, old refrigerators, recliners and other furniture, mattresses, sunken motor boats, safes, toilets, countless plastic objects, metal pieces, wood planks, and garbage are pulled, yanked, and hauled from U.S. rivers and bays each year. Projects to clean up shorelines are annual events along the east and west coasts and the Gulf of Mexico.

Cleanups include many young people, such as the Earth Conservation Corps that works to restore the Ancostia River in southeast Washington, D.C. Some other examples include the following:

- In 2009, Cumberland County, Pennsylvania, teenagers helped clean up Chesapeake Bay.
- After a dam broke in Lake Delhi, Iowa, in 2010, the flooding washed away homes, docks, furniture, boats, and many other items and left debris along the banks of the Maquoketa River. When spring arrived in 2011, a group of seniors from West Delaware High School cleaned a portion of the river bank.
- In 2010, Girl Scouts in Tampa, Florida, decided to have an environmental impact on their community by cleaning up an intercoastal waterway. The troop removed trash and recycled what they could. They also launched a canoe to pick up trash in the water as well as on the beach.
- In 2009, high school students cleaned up a half-mile stretch of the south branch of the Rahway River near Cooper Field in Iselin, New Jersey, removing trash ranging from bicycles to an entire car frame.

Off the Bookshelf

For lots of ideas about how to clean up and protect waterways, check out the book *Going Blue: A Teen Guide to Saving Our Oceans, Lakes, Rivers, and Wetlands* (2010) by Cathryn Berger Kaye and Philippe Cousteau, grandson of the famous ocean explorer Jacques Cousteau. The book describes the many threats to water sources and is a guide for service learning in five stages—investigating, preparing, acting, reflecting, and demonstrating. It also provides important facts and statistics about the earth's oceans and waterways. In addition, the views of young people are included.

- Over a five-week period in 2011, forty-three teenagers traveled through Oregon along the coast, Rogue River wilderness, and other nature areas to clean up waterways, beaches, and trails.
- During the spring of 2011 in north Florida, 129 high school students cleaned shorelines from Ponte Vedra Beach to St. Augustine, collecting nearly 7,000 pieces of trash.

Marine Debris

The EPA says that marine debris is an increasing problem along shorelines, and in coastal waters, estuaries, and oceans throughout the world. Marine debris consists of human-made waste material that is generated on land or at sea. Think about rubbish in the streets. When it rains, trash can wash into sewers, storm drains, or inland rivers and streams and can be carried to oceans and coastal waters. At sea, large fishing nets are sometimes lost or discarded, and ships and recreational boats may intentionally or accidentally dump trash directly into the ocean.

Cargo ships have lost containers during storms, dumping products into the sea. In 1992, containers of yellow rubber ducks and other bathtub toys—green

Volunteers clear a pond of debris.

frogs, blue turtles, and red beavers—fell off a Chinese freighter on its way to Washington State. Some of those items washed up on U.S. shores from Alaska to Maine, and that prompted journalist Donovan Hohn and others to try to learn more about what happened to the toys. As a result, Hohn wrote *Moby-Duck: The True Story of 28,800 Bath Toys Lost at Sea and of the Beachcombers, Oceanographers, Environmentalists, and Fools, Including the Author, Who Went in Search of Them.* Published in 2011, the book not only describes places where the toys were found but also includes much about marine science and the environmental problems of marine debris.

Whatever its source, ocean debris creates hazards for sea animals, fish, and waterfowl. Many animals get entangled in plastic netting, fishing lines, six-pack rings, and binding straps, which cause death. For example, seal pups are curious and often poke their heads into six-pack rings, which they cannot remove. Then as the seals grow the rings become collars or belts of death, slowly

See This Flick: *Waterlife*

Directed by Kevin McMahon, *Waterlife* (2010) is a documentary about the Great Lakes: Lake Superior, Lake Michigan, Lake Huron, Lake Erie, and Lake Ontario. It has been called an "epic cinematic poem that reveals the extraordinary beauty and complex toxicity of the Great Lakes,"[13] which are interconnected and together comprise the earth's last great supply of fresh drinking water. The film follows the flow of water from Lake Superior to the Atlantic Ocean and shows how the lives of 35 million people as well as aquatic life are affected by the lakes. As the film documents, the Great Lakes are under assault from a deadly combination of industrial toxins, sewage, invasive species, climate change, and profound apathy. Scientists predict that the Great Lakes ecosystem is in danger of collapse.

choking or squeezing the life out of them. Plastic bags, gloves, and sheeting in the water resemble jellyfish or other prey to some marine life. Autopsies of dead turtles and whales have revealed plastic bags in their stomachs. Plastic pellets floating on the water or washing up on beaches look like eggs, and sea birds ingest them and other small plastic objects and die of suffocation or internal blockage.

The largest area of ocean debris is the Great Pacific Garbage Patch—a floating trash heap. It is hundreds of miles wide situated in the North Pacific between Japan and California in what is called the North Pacific Subtropical Gyre. A gyre is a spiral of seawater that forms when currents smash together. Warm water from the South Pacific collides with the colder northern water, creating the whirlpool. When trash floats in the ocean and reaches the gyre, it whirls around in the garbage patch, most of which is plastic that does not decompose. Various estimates have suggested that the garbage patch is the size of Texas, but no one actually knows how large it is because it is made up of areas of trash that are underwater or spread out over many miles. And how to clean it up is another question.[14]

Because 80 percent of the trash comes from land sources, cleaning up shorelines—not just ocean beaches but also river and lake shores—is one way to reduce the trash that can end up in sea waters. It is also an important aspect of living green.

The BP Oil Spill

When the BP Deepwater Horizon oil rig in the Gulf of Mexico exploded in April 2010, eleven workers were killed and oil spewed from a deep-sea well, polluting "4,000 square miles of ocean surface, over ten times the area of New York City."[15] Across the United States and in other countries, people organized to help save the wildlife hurt by the oil spill. For example, three high school girls in Clear Lake, Iowa, held a garage and bake sale to earn funds for the National Wildlife Federation, which helped restore the habitats of coastal wildlife. One of the teenagers notes it was better to help the federation save wildlife than to buy something for themselves.

Teenager Matt Pierce, who lives in Bradenton, Florida, and in Stone Harbor, New Jersey, in the summer, initiated a fund-raising organization called Teenagers Care in 2010. The money collected helps organizations and groups that rehabilitate wildlife damaged by the BP oil spill. He was motivated by seeing photographs of pelicans covered in oil. As he puts it:

We have a local Wetlands Institute in Stone Harbor where my brother Kevin has volunteered and we see a lot of wildlife and really felt we needed to do something about the oil-sickened animals in the Gulf. We get turtles in our yard all the time and see incredible birds and dolphins in Stone Harbor. Sarasota Bay near our house in Bradenton is an amazing place with pelicans, dolphins, and many other animals. . . . I can't imagine oil on our beaches in Florida and Stone Harbor. When I see what has happened in the Gulf it makes me really wonder what we should be doing to help with our country's energy problem. My generation has now seen the result of what can happen from off-shore drilling and why we need to find alternative energy sources.[16]

Notes

1. Kyle Dresback, "Nease IB Students Clean Up St. Johns County Shores," *Florida Times-Union*, April 26, 2011, http://jacksonville.com/community/st-johns/2011-04-26/story/nease-ib-students-clean-st-johns-county-shores (accessed June 16, 2011).

2. Charles Fishman, "The Revenge of Water," from *The Big Thirst*, *The Week*, July 29, 2011, p. 40.

3. "What Is a Watershed?" *U.S. Environmental Protection Agency*, November 17, 2009, http://water.epa.gov/type/watersheds/whatis.cfm (accessed June 16, 2011).

4. National Park Service/U.S. Department of Interior, "Mississippi River Facts," December 2, 2010, www.nps.gov/miss/riverfacts.htm (accessed June 16, 2011).

5. Natalie Everett, "Teens Conserve Water, Win Scholarship," *The Santa Clarita Valley Signal*, February 22, 2010, www.the-signal.com/archives/25031 (accessed June 16, 2011).

6. Staci Matlock, "Students Test Rio Grande Water Quality," *The New Mexican*, October 8, 2010, www.santafenewmexican.com/localnews/River-gets-a-checkup (accessed June 16, 2011).

7. Jenny Shalant, "Fishing for Pollution on the Bronx River," *OnEarth Magazine*, February 8, 2010, www.onearth.org/article/fishing-for-pollution-on-the-bronx-river-947 (accessed June 11, 2011).

8. Rocking the Boat, "In Their Words: Reflections from Rocking the Boat Students," n.d. http://rockingtheboat.org/about/reflections (accessed June 11, 2011).

9. Jim Kavanaugh, "Here's the Scoop on Skimming Trash from Waterways," *CNN*, May 22, 2009, www.cnn.com/2009/TECH/05/22/scoop.invention (accessed June 14, 2011).

10. Earth Force, "GREEN Students Win the Great Indy Butt Out Contest," *earthforce.org*, May 11, 2009, http://earthforce.forumone.com/content/article/detail/2310 (accessed June 18, 2011).

11. Cameron Macdonald, "Relief for the Creeks," *Elk Grove Citizen Online*, April 22, 2011, www.egcitizen.com/articles/2011/04/22/news/doc4dae1cd87d91c018742032.txt (accessed June 11, 2011).

12. Clay M., "How You Can Save the Wetlands," *Teen Ink*, n.d., www.teenink.com/hot_topics/environment/article/268065/How-You-Can-Save-the-Wetlands (accessed June 12, 2011).

13. Bullfrogfilms, *Waterlife*, 2009, www.bullfrogfilms.com/catalog/wlife.html (accessed November 8, 2011).

14. Russell McLendon, "What Is the Great Pacific Ocean Garbage Patch?" *Mother Nature Network*, February 24, 2010, www.mnn.com/earth-matters/translating-uncle-sam/stories/what-is-the-great-pacific-ocean-garbage-patch (accessed June 15, 2011).

15. "Gulf Oil Spill," *National Geographic Channel*, n.d., http://channel.nationalgeographic.com/episode/gulf-oil-spill-5488/facts (accessed July 11, 2011).

16. "Teenager Matt Pierce Starts a Non-Profit Called Teenagers Care to Fundraise for Animals Suffering from the Gulf Oil Spill," *PR Newswire*, July 16, 2010, www.prnewswire.com/news-releases/teenager-matt-pierce-starts-a-non-profit-called-teenagers-care-to-fundraise-for-animals-suffering-from-the-gulf-oil-spill-98593534.html (accessed June 4, 2011).

HELPING PARKS, ZOOS, AND ANIMAL SANCTUARIES

"If we truly care for the health and welfare of our neighborhoods, then we must respect
and commit to helping both the human and animal members of our communities."
—Alexis Ulrich, 2010 Humane Teen of the Year[1]

Green efforts to protect wildlife and save water resources often merge with projects to clean and restore parks nationwide. Kayla Kopke, a Wayne State University (Michigan) student who attended an Earth Day 2009 event, says, "I love cleaning up parks; especially when you have a big crew. . . . You can make a big difference. There is nothing better I could be doing."[2] National, state, and local public parks across the United States sponsor cleanup or maintenance activities that draw thousands of teenagers as well as adults, not just on Earth Day but also numerous times during the year.

Maintaining National and State Parks

National parks are symbols of U.S. history and sites of historical importance as well as places of natural beauty and wildlife. The National Park Service (NPS) of the U.S. Department of Interior is responsible for maintaining the fifty-eight national parks, plus many memorial sites, parkways, reserves, rivers, and trails that are considered national park units. The NPS says that the "National Park

System comprises 394 areas covering more than 84 million acres in every state (except Delaware), the District of Columbia, American Samoa, Guam, Puerto Rico, and the Virgin Islands. These areas include national parks, monuments, battlefields, military parks, historical parks, historic sites, lakeshores, seashores, recreation areas, scenic rivers and trails, and the White House."

Tourists have enjoyed America's national parks for generations, yet the NPS says, "National parks are in disrepair. Historic buildings are crumbling, native species are losing the fight to invasive species, trails are disappearing." Invasives pose a threat to the balance of desired flora and forests in ecosystems. Nonnative plants overcrowd, compete, and, if left unattended, can completely destroy food supplies for native wildlife. On their website the NPS appeals to young people to join the Youth Conservation Corps (YCC): "Get paid to live in and help out your national parks."[3] More than a dozen national parks from Maryland to California offer YCC programs, which are designed for youth fifteen to eighteen years old. Young people who qualify for the YCC program at Yosemite National Park are paid the minimum wage in California (currently $8.00 per hour) with $70 per week deducted for room and board. The participants are expected to work the full eight weeks of the program and to take part in weekend activities. Home visits are not allowed.

In Montana, work projects include repairing fences in Glacier National Park or Big Hole National Battlefield, building and maintaining trails in Red Rocks National Wildlife Refuge or Makoshika State Park, or helping with natural resource conservation on the Rocky Mountain Front.

In other YCC programs, teenagers work in marshes, such as the Horicon Marsh National Wildlife Refuge in Wisconsin. A first-timer in 2011 was Sophia Peterson, who said she got involved because "it was a job for the summer, plus I like being out in the marsh."[4]

Almost every state has opportunities for park or trail maintenance, wilderness restoration, or other green efforts. Washington State is an example. The Student Conservation Association, the University of Washington Botanic Gardens, and Seattle Parks and Recreation projects include removing nonnative invasive plants from parks. There are 9,000 miles of wilderness trails in Washington, and high school students who opt for volunteer vacations with the Washington Trails Association spend their summers maintaining backcountry trails for hikers. Teenager Seth Gremmert says, "It's really important for us to be out here, because the work we do benefits the community center around us. . . . If we didn't have hundreds of volunteers dedicating thousands of hours every year, those trails would deteriorate and it wouldn't be acceptable and then no one would get to enjoy [the wilderness]."[5]

Much of the preservation work in state parks is done by the more than 33,000 members of service and conservation corps nationwide. The corps is patterned after the Civilian Conservation Corps of the 1930s Great Depression era. While the CCC was established for unemployed males ages seventeen to twenty-eight who worked for $30 per month plus room and board, today's corps takes both male and female workers ages sixteen to twenty-five who are paid $290 weekly plus provided board and shelter in a bunkhouse or tent. They in turn work with tens of thousands of community volunteers. Most of the funding for the corps comes from the federal government and is supplemented by grants from foundations. As the recession took hold in the United States in 2008, the corps has received many more applicants than available positions.

Nineteen-year-old Hannah Ryan, however, is one corps member who found a spot with the seven-member crew of the Canyon Country Youth Corps. Members are working in the grassland flats—open grazing areas—of the Colorado Plateau in a program to protect desert ecosystems. In May 2011 they were fencing football field–sized enclosures to prevent cows from trampling and grazing on the lands. Ryan said she applied for the two-month stint because she "wanted fulfilling work, and to see some of the Southwest, because this place is so beautiful. . . . It's hard work, but it feels good when you're done." She hopes to have a career in some type of natural resource preservation.[6]

The Virginia State Parks Youth Corps (VSPYC) involves teens who take part in trail restoration and construction. In addition, VSPYC projects include preservation of wildlife habitats, watershed work, removal of nonnative plants, and other maintenance of public lands. The parks department also sponsors a residential program called the Youth Conservation Corps, which comprises crews of ten members, ages fourteen to seventeen, supervised by college-age or older leaders. They live in the park for three weeks and work on park development and maintenance projects that include restoration and preservation of wetlands, stream banks, endangered species, and other wildlife habitats; water testing; removal of nonnative plants; and trail construction. At the end of their service, they receive a payment of $500.

From April 1 to the end of November 2011, Missouri youth, seventeen to twenty-one years of age, who were part of the State Parks Youth Corps worked in the state's eighty-five parks and historic sites. One teenager explains, "We did a lot of weed whacking, a little bit of cleanup . . . anything that needs to be done."[7]

Local Projects

If there are no positions available in service-learning conservation programs at the national or state level, local projects always need help. Many high school and college youth get involved. Consider these examples:

- More than two hundred students in Hoboken, New Jersey, participated in the Stevens Community Service Day in April 2011. They cleaned up four parks and prepared thirteen tree pits around Hoboken for the planting of new trees in May.
- New York City held its My Park Day in May 2011 at 175 park locations. More than 9,000 people, including local high school students, participated, cleaning garden beds, planting flowers, pulling weeds, painting benches and light poles, collecting trash, and generally sprucing up their neighborhood parks in the city's five boroughs.
- In Hamilton County, Indiana, students helped pull out bush honeysuckle and garlic mustard from Cool Creek Park. According to the parks

department, controlling these invasive plants is a never-ending job, so help is needed during the growing season.

- Mormon teenagers and other church volunteers in Ventura County, California, helped clean parks, area beaches, and Santa Monica Mountain trails in May 2010. In one park, the volunteers "pruned shrubs and trees, cleared invasive weeds, trimmed overgrown oak trees, rebuilt fences, cleared brush, and created and widened several trails."[8]

- The Green Teens in Lake Oswego, Oregon, "adopted" Bryant Woods Nature Park for ivy (an invasive species) removal, as well as participated in ivy removal at Tryon Creek State Park in Portland in 2010.

- In Milwaukee, Wisconsin, students joined a group of volunteers to clean up area parks in April 2010. They removed invasive species and cleaned up ball fields and the banks of the Milwaukee River. One student says, "I'm just finding a lot of plastic wrappers, food wrappers; there's a lot of broken glass laying around, a lot of beer cans."[9]

- Teenagers in Muskogee, Oklahoma, who are members of Students Working Against Tobacco, joined the Youth Volunteer Corps at city parks in 2011 to clean up discarded tobacco products—cigarette butts, cigar remainders, and chewing tobacco tins. According to student Derra Walker, after the cleanup the students took the tobacco debris to the Muskogee City Council "so they can see how it affects the city."[10]

Protecting Wolves

Tourists at some national parks such as Yellowstone often visit sites where they can see animals in the wild, such as grizzly bears, bison, coyotes, elk, and gray wolves. But to farmers and ranchers, wolves long have been considered vicious killers of cows, sheep, and other livestock. Hunters also condemn wolves for killing elk, deer, and other game animals. Thus, wolves have been shot, poisoned, and trapped to near extinction.

Indian Land or Public Land?

Whether at the national, state, or local level, Americans long have debated where parks should be located, how they should be used, and who should have access. For example, Native American tribes have strongly objected to the establishment of some national or state parks on reservation land or sacred sites. Consider the group of young Native Americans from several tribes who converged in 1970 at Mount Rushmore National Memorial, part of the Black Hills National Parks in South Dakota. The group was there to aid the Sioux Nation in a protest and an effort to take back the Black Hills from the U.S. government. Although authorities tried to stop them, the group climbed to the top of the mountain and hung a flag proclaiming Sioux Indian power near the carved faces of four U.S. presidents. Over the decades since 1970, an annual commemoration is held to remember the takeover of Mount Rushmore.

A more recent protest took place in April 2011, when Native Americans occupied a waterfront area known as Glen Cove in Vallejo, California, where the recreation district planned to spend $1.5 million to develop a park. Indians claim the area was once an ancient Ohlone village, Sogorea Tea, and burial site. Protestors set up a tent and built a sacred fire for their spiritual encampment. Their vigil was joined in June 2011 by runners who take part in the annual five-hundred-mile American Indian Spiritual Marathon. The marathon was initiated in 1978 as a means to convey the message that all life is sacred and that humans need to maintain a balance with Mother Earth.

Because wolves naturally prey on elk, keeping a balance in the herds, elk and deer became so numerous in parks that they were destroying ecosystems by foraging on trees, plants, and in meadows. When the wolves became nearly extinct, the elk and deer populations grew.

Since the 1970s, gray wolves have been protected under the Endangered Species Act (ESA) of 1973, a federal law that provides for the conservation of species that

It Happened to Maine Skateboarders

Skateboarding is considered a green mode of travel, and there are some thirteen million skateboarders in the United States. But skateboarders who practice their tricks at any convenient spot in towns and cities are not necessarily welcome. So a group of teenagers in Bucksport, Maine, began a project in May 2011 to create its own skateboard park. The town's officials gave the group permission to use an ice-skating rink until winter. The teens set up a homemade ramp and other objects that they can slide or jump over or maneuver. But they hoped to create their own park with the aid of town supporters. Eighteen-year-old Allan Abott notes that townspeople "don't want us on the streets 'cause they think we're causing trouble." The police chief agrees and supports the need for the park so the teens can enjoy their sport. Eighteen-year-old Ryan Nevells says, "It's just like any other sport. . . . It's just something we like doing."[11]

are in danger of becoming extinct or are threatened with extinction throughout all or a significant portion of their range. In 1995 and 1996, Canadian wolf packs with breeding pairs were reintroduced to Yellowstone and central Idaho (which is primarily U.S. Forest Service land), resulting in a controversy over the increase in wolf populations. "Kill the wolves!" is the cry of ranchers, hunters, and some residents near the park boundaries. "Save the wolves!" is the call of such groups as Defenders of Wildlife, the Western Wildlife Conservancy, and the National Wildlife Federation, as well as biologists and environmentalists.

In 2008, the U.S. Department of the Interior removed the northern Rockies gray wolf from the endangered species list. States in that region—Montana, Wyoming, and Idaho, and parts of Washington, Utah, and Oregon—are expected to manage their wolf populations. That has not pleased environmentalists and others who believe conservation is part of living green. In fact, Oregon's management plan included nonlethal methods for preventing wolf attacks, but the state has issued

Did You Know?

Yellowstone National Park was the first national park. Established in 1872, it covers areas in Wyoming, Montana, and Idaho and is home to a large variety of wildlife, including grizzly bears, wolves, bison, and elk. Old Faithful and a collection of the world's most extraordinary geysers and hot springs and the Grand Canyon of the Yellowstone also are located in the park.

permits allowing landowners to kill wolves that prey on dogs or livestock. The state in mid-2011 had a wolf population of only seventeen.

In the western Great Lakes region, gray wolves also were endangered and were protected by the ESA, but now they far outnumber those in the northern Rockies. According to the U.S. Department of Interior's Fish and Wildlife Service, more than four thousand gray wolves were counted in Minnesota, Wisconsin, and Michigan's Upper Peninsula during the winter of 2009–2010. Thus, the Department of Interior announced in May 2011 that gray wolves in the western Great Lakes area would be removed from the list of endangered and threatened species because wolves have recovered in this area and no longer require the protection of the ESA.

Saving Endangered Species

Along with wolves, the bald eagle, brown pelican, and whooping crane are other creatures that have been placed on the U.S. endangered species list and, after recovery, were removed. Currently in the United States, there are more than 1,900 species listed as endangered under the ESA, which could protect them from becoming extinct.

Long before the ESA became law, some species disappeared. Since the 1600s, more than five hundred plants and animals have become extinct in North America.

Consider the passenger pigeon. In North America, the birds were so numerous a century ago that it was common to see flocks of thousands flying overhead. Now there is not a single passenger pigeon alive. They disappeared because so many of their habitats—forests—were cut down and because they often were shot for food.

The International Union for Conservation of Nature (IUCN) keeps track of species worldwide that are vulnerable, threatened with extinction, endangered, or critically endangered. The IUCN notes that more amphibian species are under threat than any single animal group. Of the nearly 10,000 bird species that have been categorized, more than 1,200 are listed as threatened or endangered.

Why should anyone care about the loss of species, whatever they happen to be? In the first place, no creature exists all alone. We are all part of a complex network of life, and the disappearance of a single species can affect many others— including humans. Saving a species may result in benefits for agriculture, industry, and human health. The U.S. Fish and Wildlife Service notes:

> Every species contains a unique storehouse of genetic material that has evolved over eons of time. Once lost, this cannot be retrieved or duplicated. Scientists have only partially investigated about 2 percent of the more than 250,000 known plant species for possible medicinal values. The chemical secrets of most species have yet to be unraveled for potential benefits. . . . A fungus that originally gave us the anti-bacterial medicines penicillin and cyclosporin A has dramatically increased the success of organ transplant operations. The compound taxol was first isolated from the bark of the Pacific yew, a small tree of America's old-growth forests in the Pacific Northwest. Taxol has been found to be an effective treatment for ovarian, breast, and other types of cancer. Nearly 40 percent of all medical prescriptions dispensed annually in the United States are derived from nature or synthesized to mimic naturally occurring chemical compounds.[12]

The American bald eagle, a national symbol, was once on the endangered species list but has recovered.

Zoos—Conserving or Imprisoning Animals?

The Little Rock (Arkansas) Zoo declares it is "committed to the conservation of endangered and threatened species in the wild" by "educating the public about wildlife conservation and supporting programs that help save threatened and endangered animals in the wild."[13] The Pittsburgh (Pennsylvania) Zoo's website says, "Everything we do at The Pittsburgh Zoo and PPG Aquarium has conservation at its roots."[14] The Phoenix (Arizona) Zoo says it "strives to be a leader in Living Green."[15] A blog about living green is the way the Cincinnati (Ohio) Zoo presents its eco-friendly tips.

It has been common in modern times for zoo supporters to define zoos as educational places with opportunities to learn about many animals and nature. As is frequently the case, many city dwellers will never see wild animals, birds, reptiles, and aquatic life except at zoos. Supporters also say that zoos can inspire young people to careers ranging from biology to zoology.

Yet, zoo opponents, such as animal-rights activists, contend that animals should live in freedom in their natural habitat and not in cages or enclosed spaces for the entertainment of humans. Some suggest closing all zoos and saving as much of the wild as possible. Writing for *Teen Ink*, a young author from Honolulu, Hawaii, opines:

> The practice of confining wild animals in zoos is appalling and should be abolished. Certainly many zoos aim to educate and emphasize the needs of animals as well as the importance of conservation to its visitors. A majority of zoos include sign posts or brochures regarding information on animal species, behaviors, and other miscellaneous facts. However, this form of education is very general and deficient; the only way to properly understand an animal is by seeing it in its natural environment. By isolating animals from their ecosystem, zoos give a misleading and artificial interpretation of an animal's true nature.[16]

It's a Fact

The forerunners of zoological gardens and zoos date back to the Middle Ages, when royal families collected wild "exotic" animals in a menagerie, or a place of captivity, located in palace gardens. The royals maintained the menagerie for their own pleasure and curiosity and as a means of displaying their wealth. But in the 1700s, menageries became traveling exhibits, and showmen with a flair displayed the animals for ordinary folks. When such tours took place in eighteenth-century America, the exotic animals included elephants, camels, lions, tigers, monkeys, and parrots.

In spite of debates, zoos across the United States attract millions of visitors. Most seek volunteer teenagers, usually between the ages of fourteen and eighteen, to provide a variety of services, such as interacting with zoo guests and teaching young children about animals. Summer volunteer programs provide teenagers with hands-on experiences dealing with animal husbandry and also teaching visitors about animal conservation efforts.

Sanctuaries for Pets and Farm Animals

Saving lives is what many animal shelters are all about, and it is common for animal lovers to volunteer to help protect homeless and/or abused or neglected pets in these facilities. In some cases, though, actions for animal welfare go beyond the walls of a shelter. Horse lovers may volunteer to work at sanctuaries that care for abused and neglected horses and those scheduled for slaughter or at sanctuaries for injured or sick wild horses that will be reintroduced to their own habitat and herd. Other sanctuaries care for farm animals that have not been treated humanely, exotic birds, circus animals that are no longer wanted by their owners, and wildlife. Almost every state has some type of sanctuary for animal, fowl, reptile, or bird protection.

Federal and state laws also exist to protect and prevent cruelty to animals, but

Monkey Business

Beginning about 2009, a rhesus macaque monkey has been on the loose in Florida around the Tampa Bay area, possibly within fifty-square miles. As of June 23, 2011, the male monkey was still a fugitive. Dubbed the "mystery monkey," its origin is unknown, but it could have been someone's illegal pet or an escapee from a state park in central Florida, where a monkey colony has existed since the 1930s. Residents in the Tampa area have photographed the monkey in their backyard trees, on their pool enclosures, and even out on city streets. But no one has been able to catch the mystery monkey—not even a professional wildlife trapper, who has hit the creature with tranquilizer darts.

Mystery monkey is so cleverly elusive that he has gained thousands of fans on Facebook and has been featured in TV news stories and on Stephen Colbert's comedy show. Fans do not want "their" monkey captured and hope he can hang on to his freedom. One follower in Pinellas County has videoed the monkey, a regular visitor. The videographer submitted photos to the *St. Petersburg Times* but asked to remain anonymous in order to protect the monkey. As he tells the newspaper reporter in an e-mail,

I took the video from inside the house as [the monkey] is very shy and will take off in a heartbeat if he sees movement inside. . . . He has a couple of acres of woods to hang out in with no one to bother him. There are many critters that live here . . . all wild except for my cat . . . but this is the first monkey and it is a hoot to see him swing thru the trees on vines like Tarzan.[17]

sometimes those laws are not strictly enforced. A *Humane Teen* member, Theresa, writes that she and a friend have

been working on an ongoing project involving puppy mills. . . . We helped pass legislation in Washington State that provides requirements for mass breeding facilities (passed in April of 2009, SB 5651). We're planning to continue making some presentations to kids at local schools to spread the word about puppy mills and overpopulation and inspire kids to take action. . . . I think it's so cruel and wrong that humans are mass-producing animals and exploiting their bodies, whether to produce offspring, inject them with Botox in labs, or force them to produce products for us to eat [as in factory farming].[18]

Another high-schooler, Jordan, in Needham, Massachusetts, also took political action. He notes:

When I was a freshman in high school, I filed House Bill 344, with Coalition to Protect and Rescue Pets to ban devocalization in MA. Devocalization is the cruel practice of cutting a dog's or cat's vocal cords just to stifle his voice. It's cruel, dangerous, and more common than you would think. The bill was fought hard by special interests with a lot of money that profit from devocalization, working to kill the bill or amend it to make the law unenforceable and useless. Fortunately, they failed. The bill was signed by Gov. Deval Patrick on April 22, 2010, after 16 months.[19]

To earn his Eagle Scout rank, teenager Matt Saginario took on a project for Farm Sanctuary near his home in Horseheads, New York. Farm Sanctuary in Watkins Glen, New York, was founded in 1986 to combat the abuses of industrialized farming or factory farming in which animals are confined in warehouse-like facilities until slaughtered for food. Matt's project involved building a jungle gym for rescued goats at the Farm Sanctuary. Goats like to climb and the gym provided a wooden structure for that activity.

Teenager Alexandra Joy Gritta is a published author of books about the inhumane treatment of horses. She writes:

At my book signings I try to make as many people as I can aware of the shipment of American horses across U.S. borders to Canada and Mexico for slaughter. Americans do not even eat horse meat, yet slaughter buyers attend our auctions, buy our horses and transport them in inhumane ways to slaughter them in other countries. I believe that if horses have been born and/or bred on American soil then we owe them more respect and protection than that.

The inhumane transport and slaughter of American horses for human consumption bothers me a lot. I also believe that all animals, whether they are domestic or livestock, deserve our respect, basic care and a good quality of life. Many animals on this planet are here only because humans breed them. If we create these lives, we should take full responsibility for the quality of lives these animals lead.

Alexandra donates all the profits from her books to "organizations that provide safe habitats and new homes for horses, rescue them during disasters, help relocate them when they are stolen, and provide humane retirement for them."[20]

Alexis Ulrich, Humane Teen of the Year in 2010 who has spoken out against the cruel slaughter of Canadian seals, is also a long-time advocate for animal protection elsewhere. A student at the University of Colorado, Denver, Alexis has established an animal club on campus and has expanded her knowledge about international animal laws and how people can work locally to bring about humane policies and legislation for animals. In her view, as noted in the opening quote, "If we truly care for the health and welfare of our neighborhoods, then we must respect and commit to helping both the human and animal members of our communities."[21]

Notes

1. Humane Society, "Educating Classmates about Animal Cruelty Is Key for '2010 Humane Teen of the Year,'" press release, February 8, 2010, www.humanesociety.org/news/press_releases/2010/02/2010_humane_teen_020810.html (accessed June 25, 2011).
2. Santiago Esparza, "Earth Day Activities Begin Early," *Detroit-LISC*, April 18, 2009, www

.detroit-lisc.org/news/908 (accessed June 17, 2011).

3. "Youth Conservation Corps," *National Park Service*, n.d., www.nps.gov/gettinginvolved/youthprograms/ycc.htm (accessed June 18, 2011).

4. Megan Sheridan, "Teens Reap Rewards from Conservation Corps Involvement," *Beaver Dam Daily Citizen*, June 17, 2011, www.wiscnews.com/bdc/news/local/article_c76a74b8-9957-11e0-a585-001cc4c03286.html (accessed June 22, 2011).

5. "Volunteer Vacations for Teens," video, *Washington Trails Association*, uploaded April 23, 2008, www.youtube.com/watch?v=AtQMVWzw7JY (accessed June 19, 2011).

6. Brandon Loomis, "S. Utah Program Trains Young Workers for Outdoor Careers," *Salt Lake Tribune*, May 1, 2011, www.sltrib.com/csp/cms/sites/sltrib/pages/printerfriendly.csp?id=51636326 (accessed June 19, 2011).

7. "State Parks Youth Corps," *MO.gov*, n.d., www.mo.gov/working-in-missouri/state-parks-youth-corps (accessed June 19, 2011).

8. Michele Willer-Allred, "Church Volunteers Put in Day Cleaning Parks," *Ventura County Star*, May 8, 2010, www.vcstar.com/news/2010/may/08/church-volunteers-put-in-day-cleaning-parks (accessed June 18, 2011).

9. "Local Volunteers Clean Up Parks, Waterways," video, *WISN*, uploaded April 17, 2010, www.youtube.com/watch?v=lIpK2J1yTCM (accessed June 20, 2011).

10. Keith Purtell, "SWAT and Muskogee Youth Volunteer Corps Join to Clean Up Parks and Playgrounds," *Muskogee Phoenix*, July 11, 2011, http://muskogeephoenix.com/local/x1227517242/SWAT-and-Muskogee-Youth-Volunteer-Corps-join-to-clean-up-parks-and-playgrounds (accessed July 12, 2011).

11. Rich Hewitt, "Teens Organize to Create Skate Park," *Bangor (Maine) Daily News*, May 9, 2011, http://bangordailynews.com/2011/05/09/news/teens-organize-to-create-skate-park (accessed June 20, 2011).

12. "Why Saving Endangered Species Matters," *U.S. Fish and Wildlife Service Endangered Species Program*, February 2002, www.fws.gov/asheville/pdfs/Why_Save_Endangered_Species.pdf (accessed July 13, 2011).

13. "Conservation," *LittleRockZoo.com*, n.d., www.littlerockzoo.com/conservation (accessed June 24, 2011).

14. "Zoo Green Initiatives," *Pittsburgh Zoo and PPG Aquarium*, n.d., http://zoo.pgh.pa.us/Conservation/LivingGreen/ZooGreenInitiatives (accessed June 24, 2011).

15. "Going Green," *Phx Zoo*, n.d., www.phoenixzoo.org/support/help/be_green.shtml (accessed June 24, 2011).

16. Worldpeace, "Open Your Eyes to the Reality of Zoos," *Teen Ink*, n.d., www.teenink.com/hot_topics/environment/article/309877/Open-Your-Eyes-to-the-Reality-of-Zoos (accessed June 23, 2011).

17. Emily Nipps, "Mystery Monkey Caught on Tape," *St. Petersburg Times*, June 23, 2011, www.tampabay.com/news/bizarre/mystery-monkey-caught-on-tape/1176935 (accessed June 24, 2011).

18. "Theresa," *Humane Teen*, n.d., www.humaneteen.org/?q=node/1179 (accessed June 24, 2011).

19. "Jordan," *Humane Teen*, n.d., www.humaneteen.org/?q=node/1294 (accessed June 24, 2011).

20. "Alexandra Joy Gritta," *Humane Teen*, n.d., www.humaneteen.org/?q=node/1258 (accessed July 20, 2011).

21. Humane Society, "Educating Classmates about Animal Cruelty Is Key for '2010 Humane Teen of the Year,'" press release, February 8, 2010, www.humanesociety.org/news/press_releases/2010/02/2010_humane_teen_020810.html (accessed June 25, 2011).

CONSERVING AND PLANTING TREES AND GARDENS

· ·

*"Planting trees really makes communities more beautiful and meeting other people who
care about the environment is always fun."*
—Nicole Coakley, a Boston, Massachusetts, high school student[1]

Living green is literally what trees and gardens do naturally, but planting them and keeping them green is a job for many environmentally conscious people. Saving trees can be an especially difficult undertaking, as lumber companies in the United States and other countries cut great swaths of forests to supply lumber for construction or wood pulp for paper manufacturing or to clear land for agriculture. Yet forest conservation does have a long history in the United States.

For example, in 1875 conservationists formed the American Forestry Association to promote the value of forests. American conservationist John Muir established the Sierra Club in 1892 to protect the habitat of the Sierra Nevada range with its forests, woodlands, and lakes. By the early 1900s, a National Park Service with authority to protect federal forests within national parks had been established. Throughout the twentieth century, public officials and private conservationists became increasingly aware of the value of preserving standing woodlands and forests.

What are some of those values? Trees keep soil from eroding and help prevent the transport of sediment and chemicals into streams. Trees hold moisture in the ground and provide habitats for birds and diverse animals. Also, they frequently

> ! **More Carbon**
>
> ⊙ Deforestation adds extra carbon dioxide to the atmosphere. That's because living trees absorb carbon and store it in their trunks, branches, leaves, and roots. When people cut down forests to build homes, farms, and roads, fewer trees are left to absorb carbon. The extra carbon in the atmosphere further enhances the greenhouse effect. Sometimes people cut trees and then burn the remaining stumps to clear land for farming. Burning trees releases even more carbon dioxide into the air.

are filters for air pollutants and help cut energy consumption by protecting buildings from the hot sun and cold winds. Trees are "sinks," or holding places, for carbon dioxide and help reduce carbon footprints. Trees around buildings absorb sound and significantly reduce noise levels from outdoor traffic and other activities.

With all the benefits that trees provide, it would seem logical to conserve and use them wisely. But because consumers worldwide demand many types of wood or wood-based products, those interests are in conflict with conservationists. These conflicts have become heated and sometimes violent in temperate forest regions in the United States and Canada and in tropical rain forest regions of the world.

Old-Growth Debates

Some of the most contentious issues arise in the Pacific Northwest, where "old-growth" and mature forests are located in the area from southeast Alaska and southwest British Columbia, down through western Washington, western Oregon, and the edge of northern California and from the Pacific Ocean inland to the crest of the Cascade Mountains.[2] According to the U.S. Department of Agriculture, there are more than ten million acres of old-growth forests in Washington, Oregon, and California. Some of the old-growth trees are more than 1,000 years old, while others are several hundred to 750 years old.

What Is a Tree Hugger?

When the term *tree hugger* originated, it was used by loggers and others to disparage those who were against timber industries. "Go hug a tree if you think it's so great!" was the challenge. And some environmentalists took that seriously. Activists have linked arms and encircled trees in order to prevent timber companies from cutting them down. Some radical environmentalists have gone beyond that protective measure and have driven spikes into trees, making them unsuitable for timber, or they have sabotaged machinery used by timber companies. However, most environmentalists today work to persuade the public and government agencies that forestlands and woods should be preserved and managed sustainably; they proudly assume the "tree hugger" label.

Although logging companies cut timber primarily on private lands, the U.S. Forest Service allows commercial logging in some public forestland with the rationale that removing some trees reduces fire hazards, improves habitats, and provides needed jobs. When logging companies cut timber on forestlands, they often use clear-cut methods, which strip wide sections of forestland, frequently causing soil erosion and pollution of streams.

Clear-cutting led to a major controversy over the fate of the Northern Spotted Owl, which was listed as an endangered species in 1990. The owls live in old-growth forests and are threatened by loss of habitat because of fragmentation of the forests. By 2011, Washington State had lost 90 percent of its old-growth forests, and the populations of the Northern Spotted Owl also dropped from 60 to 40 percent.

Conservationists try to protect forest ecosystems and wildlife habitat on both private and public land from bad logging practices, but seldom are they successful. Nevertheless, when two spotted owls were seen in mid-2010 near the Willamette National Forest in Oregon, the U.S. Forest Service barred a timber company from

It Happened to Julia "Butterfly" Hill

Julia "Butterfly" Hill was twenty-three-years old when she began her nearly two-year vigil in 1997 in the canopy of a giant redwood tree that she named Luna. Her action was part of a struggle to save the ancient redwoods in northern California. Pacific Lumber Company had been clear-cutting large areas of ancient forests, leaving barren slopes that quickly turned to mud slides during rainstorms. Julia Hill, with other activists, attempted to stop the destruction, but loggers, company guards, and some employees of the lumber company attacked verbally and intimidated them by felling giant trees close by and flying a helicopter overhead.

When Hill first became a tree sitter in the canopy in early December 1997, she expected to be there only a short time. But she stayed for weeks and months. Support crews hoisted food, drinking water, and other supplies. She had a hand-cranked radio, a cell phone, an old video camera, and writing and reading materials that included a lot of environmental articles and books.

Throughout 1998 and most of 1999, she endured periodic attacks by Pacific Lumber to force her out of Luna. She was bombarded with air horns, floodlights, and loud music. Helicopters endangered her with updrafts as they flew illegally nearby. Guards prevented volunteers from sending up food supplies, trying to starve her out. A professional climber tried to force her to abandon her platform. The weather also battered her at times with freezing rains, sleet, and high winds. She suffered frostbite.

Whatever the difficulties and near tragedies, she survived and, after months of negotiating, finally reached a legally binding agreement with the lumber company to protect Luna and create a buffer zone around the tree. Hill descended from her platform on December 18, 1999. Her book about her experiences, *The Legacy of Luna* (2000), was published soon afterward and became a best-seller.

Unfortunately, in November 2000, Hill received devastating news. After her two-year vigil, Luna had been slashed with a chainsaw. No one knew who perpetrated the act, but there were plenty of people who wanted to save Luna. According to California's nonprofit land trust Sanctuary Forest, working side by side into the night, leading arborists, engineers, biologists, and employees of Pacific Lumber Company and the California Department of Forestry volunteered to help. These experts designed, manufactured, and installed steel brackets and cables to bolster the tree through winter storms. There were predictions that Luna would show signs of dieback, but four years later in 2004 her canopy still looked green and strong. Supported by the trees around her, Luna's roots are nourished and stabilized and the 1000-year-old tree endures.[3]

logging in the area. In 2011, the Environmental Protection Information Center (EPIC) in California was able to prevent logging near a spotted owl nesting site.

Tropical Rainforest Products

Tropical rainforests are the source of numerous products that many of us consume, such as fruits and vegetables, nuts, and spices. Think about these foods: avocadoes, bananas, brazil nuts, cashew nuts, coconuts, coffee, macadamia nuts, mangoes, okra, papayas, peanuts, pineapples, plantains, and others—all connected to tropical rainforests. Major rainforest spices are cloves, nutmeg, black pepper, allspice, cardamom, ginger, vanilla, and cinnamon, worth millions of dollars in international trade.

Rainforests also provide the wood needed to manufacture such products as doors, packing cases and boxes, flooring, paneling, railroad ties, wharf pilings, cabinetry, desks, drawing boards, salad bowls, and toys. Just look around a home, school, office, store, or other building, and you could list additional products made from wood, much of which comes from rainforests.

Seldom do most people think of rainforests as the source of the ingredients for cosmetics and pharmaceuticals. Medicinal drugs derived from tropical plants may treat AIDS, cancer, diabetes, arthritis, and Alzheimer's disease. Muscle relaxants, steroids, and local anesthetics are medicinals that are plant based. Yet these biological treasures are being lost just as scientists are beginning to assess their value. They have

> identified more than 2,000 tropical plants that contain substances for treating various types of cancer. . . . One example is the rosy periwinkle found in the rainforest of Madagascar, off the southeast coast of Africa. Periwinkle's tiny pink flower is the source of two compounds: one for the treatment of childhood leukemia and another for the treatment of Hodgkin's disease.[4]

Rainforest Destruction

One and one-half acres of rainforest are lost every second, according to Rain-Tree, a nutrition company that sells products from sustainable plants of the Amazon rainforest. Rainforests once covered 14 percent of the earth's land surface; now they cover a mere 6 percent. When rainforests are destroyed, so are the habitats for more than 50 percent of the species on earth and the homes of millions of indigenous people. Centuries ago, there were an estimated ten million Indians living in the Amazonian rainforest. Today there are less than 200,000.[5]

Governments in tropical regions frequently encourage forest clearing in order to provide income from exported timber products. Forests also are cleared to create grazing land for cattle, which in turn brings in profits from meat exports. In addition, people in developing countries cut forestland to obtain wood for fuel and to farm. But the cleared land usually is not suitable for long-term farming. The soil soon loses its nutrients and erodes, so people must move on to clear even more forests.

Oil (petroleum) extraction also endangers rainforests as roads and pipelines are constructed to and from drilling sites. Hundreds of thousands of square miles of tropical forests have been destroyed by dam building in such countries as Brazil, India, and Indonesia. The dams are built to provide hydroelectric power and to support such industries as mining and foundries.

As forests are cleared, road building and bulldozing add to ecosystem damage. So do fires set to remove trees in preparation for farming, ranching, or plantation planting—that is, planting a single species of trees, such as rubber, coconut, or palm trees, for commercial harvesting of their products.

In Southeast Asia, for example, rainforests are cleared to plant palm trees, which produce palm oil used in many food products. When the Asian forests are cut down, the habitat for orangutans is destroyed, threatening the animals. That upset two teenage Girl Scouts, Rhino Tomtit and Madison Verve, in Michigan, who had studied orangutans during a project to earn a Girl Scout Bronze Award in 2007. They took action to call attention to endangered orangutans, and in the process they refused to eat foods that included palm oil as an ingredient. Then, when the time came for the annual sale of Girl Scout cookies, the girls were dismayed to find that all the varieties contained palm oil. They protested by not taking part in the cookie sale and expressing their concerns about the connection between palm oil harvests and lost orangutan habitat, rallying support from other Girl Scout troops across the United States.

The teenagers tried to contact Girl Scout officials, requesting that the cookie recipe be changed, but they were told that the palm oil was a needed ingredient to preserve taste and shelf life of the cookies. However, in the spring of 2011, Tomtit and Verve received widespread media attention when they met with Girl Scout officials who "agreed to research palm oil to determine if they can get more of the ingredient from rain forests that haven't been cleared for palm oil plantations, or if they can replace it with something else."[6]

Individuals may not be able to launch protests like the Michigan Girl Scouts, but they can help preserve rainforests by donating to or volunteering for activities of organizations like the Nature Conservancy, the Rainforest Conservation Fund, Rainforest Action Network, World Land Trust–U.S., Rainforest Foundation, and Rainforest Alliance. The latter organization established a program in 1989 called SmartWood, which certifies, through an independent third party, that wood products come from well-managed, or sustainable, forests.

> ## "Food of the Gods"
>
> One of the world's favorite foods is chocolate, which is derived from the cacao plant (*Theobroma cacao*) that grows in rainforests. Thousands of years ago, the Mayas in the region currently known as Guatemala made a bitter, spicy drink from cacao beans. They believed that the cocoa tree was a god-given gift, and thus it became the "food of the gods." When Europeans were introduced to cacao, they created a drink with processed cacao beans, cane sugar, and water. Once solid milk chocolate was developed, the popularity of chocolate increased, and today the food of the gods is considered a special gift for birthdays, holidays, and other special occasions.

Planting America's Trees

A 2010 USDA report, *Sustaining America's Urban Trees and Forests*, declares, "Close to 80 percent of the U.S. population lives in urban areas and depends on the essential ecological, economic, and social benefits provided by urban trees and forests. However, the distribution of urban tree cover and the benefits of urban forests vary across the United States, as do the challenges of sustaining this important resource."[7]

A person who is well aware of the need to sustain urban forests is Andy Lipkis. As a teenager in 1970, Andy began a crusade (and later a reforesting organization, TreePeople) that is still in existence and thriving today. When he was fifteen years old, Andy learned that trees in the forests around Los Angeles were dying because of urban smog and other pollutants in the area. In the TV series *It's Easy Being Green*, filmed in Los Angeles, Lipkis notes, "I was born and raised here in Los Angeles, and my parents' response to me being raised in the smog was to send me up to the mountains with clean air about 100 miles from here where we could play and breathe."[8] At the mountain camp, a naturalist explained that the pine forests were dying from air pollution creeping up from the city below, and the forest would disappear in a few decades unless smog-tolerant species could be planted. So Lipkis decided to do something about the problem. He mobilized a group of teenage campers, who plowed up an old parking lot and planted smog- and drought-tolerant tree seedlings. The seedlings grew and flourished, and in 1973, during his first year in college, Lipkis founded TreePeople, which currently has eight thousand members, who, since the organization's founding, have planted two million trees in the Los Angeles area.

Such groups as 4-H and organizations like the Sierra Club, Keep America Beautiful, the Wilderness Society, the National Audubon Society, the Nature Conservancy, and others engage in tree-planting programs. So do students, families, and individuals who realize that planting trees is a relatively simple way to be green and take action right in their own backyards or neighborhoods.

That was the case for three teenagers, Connor, David, and Austin of Tulsa, Oklahoma. In 2010, they started a project called Green Tree of Tulsa, which was designed to replace trees that had been destroyed by an ice storm. They tried to get help from environmental groups, but Connor reports, "It was kind of difficult at first because they thought we were just some kids just trying to take on more than we could do. . . . But once we got some accomplishments, we could say we've planted 2,000 in Tulsa, it carried some weight and they started believing in us more."[9]

Many Americans, including students from elementary school to college level, focus on tree planting on Arbor Day each year. Julius Morton originated Arbor Day more than a century ago. He had moved from the east coast to Nebraska, where there were few trees, so he encouraged German immigrants living on the prairies to plant trees, especially orchards. Morton founded the National Arbor Day Foundation, which sponsors a variety of programs to encourage tree planting, especially in urban areas.

In recent years some major cities have launched tree-planting programs in order to counteract the loss of shade trees in new developments and inadequate care of older trees. Global ReLeaf of the American Forestry Association, which

The Nation's Tree

In 2004, the U.S. Congress passed legislation designating a national tree. Was it:

A. aspen

B. birch

C. cottonwood

D. dogwood

E. elm

F. none of the above?

After a voting process sponsored by the National Arbor Day Foundation, the mighty oak won the honor, finishing with more than 101,000 votes, compared to almost 81,000 for the runner-up, the giant redwood. More than sixty species of oaks grow in the United States, and throughout the nation's history, oaks have been prized for their shade, beauty, and lumber. In a press release, U.S. senator Ben Nelson of Nebraska notes that the oak is a "fine choice to represent our nation's strength, as it grows from just an acorn into a powerful entity whose many branches continue to strengthen and reach skyward with every passing year."[10]

works to plant trees in forests, has another program called Global ReLeaf Fund, whose purpose is to plant trees in urban areas. Each dollar contributed to the fund pays for planting one tree through the ReLeaf programs.

Planting Community Gardens

Students in Chicago's Humboldt Park are "tending plants in a brand new greenhouse atop the Puerto Rican Cultural Center. The plants are then transferred

> **?** **What Do You Think? Is a Fallen Log Dead?**
>
> If you have ever taken a walk in the woods or followed a forest trail, undoubtedly you have seen or perhaps walked or sat on a fallen log. That log may look like it's dead, but its bark provides fodder for scavengers. If it's on wet land, it holds moisture, and plants and tree seedlings may take root near or inside it. Beetles like to bore holes into logs, and that allows other organisms to follow suit to find sustenance. Sometimes logs fall into streams and create pools of water where fish can spawn. A fallen log eventually may rot and disintegrate, but even then it provides nutrients for the soil and plants. So what do you think? Is a fallen log dead?

to community gardens, where they'll flourish and be distributed to residents." Their efforts are a response to the high levels of diabetes in this Puerto Rican community. Students are working in conjunction with a door-to-door campaign to educate residents about diabetes, which led student Jessie Fuentes to a "frightening discovery. She has Type 1 diabetes. 'When my uncle had diabetes his legs were amputated. When my cousin got it he went blind,' Fuentes said. 'So seeing people with diabetes growing up was never a good experience.'"[11]

Community gardens are flourishing in many urban areas from New York City to Los Angeles. Often these gardens help revitalize neighborhoods. In 2008, the city of Cleveland, Ohio, boasted a total of 188 community gardens in the city and nearby suburbs. Neighbors came together to turn vacant lots into productive vegetable gardens, and the produce, valued at over $1 million, provided fresh vegetables for the gardeners and their neighbors. Surplus vegetables went to local food banks.[12]

Through a Philadelphia program called Teens 4 Good (T4G), at-risk teenagers are provided job opportunities to convert blighted vacant lots into multipurpose urban green spaces that include urban gardens or farms. Teenagers not only learn about gardening but also develop business skills by selling the products they have

Planting trees is an activity that numerous conservation groups support.

grown. In addition, the produce provides healthy food for the urban community. Randy Butler, a 2010 participant, notes, "T4G has taught me how to garden and sell produce and it has encouraged me to be open to different jobs." Another participant, Sukesha Simpson, declares that T4G "helped me to develop some kind of career in agriculture. As a result, it has taught me to become a better person overall."[13]

Philadelphia also has a Philadelphia Orchard Project (POP), which has planted numerous orchards throughout the city "in formerly vacant lots, community gardens, schoolyards, and other spaces, almost exclusively in low-income neighborhoods where people lack access to fresh fruit." The orchards contain both trees and vines and produce such fruits as apples, cherries, figs, pawpaws, peaches, pears, persimmons, plums, blackberries, blueberries, currants, elderberries, gooseberries, grapes, and kiwis. One of the orchards supplements the vegetables that T4G grow and sell.[14]

Planting and caring for a garden helps many U.S. young people appreciate the environment and the concept of living green.

Did You Know?

Guerilla gardening is a special urban way to plant and grow a garden. It's a surreptitious method to grow foods or flowers within public plots. Vegetables or flowers might be planted in roadway median strips or along public sidewalks. Or guerilla gardeners may plant private lands, with or without the owners' permission. Often these gardeners work at night, and some tactics include tossing "mud balls," or dirt filled with seeds or seedlings, onto vacant public lands and then waiting to see what sprouts. While guerilla gardening is not legal, seldom do such gardeners get into trouble with authorities.

During the summer of 2011, teens in Takoma Park, Maryland, opted to begin a community garden on a plot next to the police department. It is an effort to offset less-desirable teen activities, such as covering walls and buildings with graffiti. The group of about two dozen teenagers planted "tomatoes, green peppers, habanera peppers, cucumbers, zucchini and oregano, among other vegetables."[15]

The U.S. Department of Agriculture (USDA) says the benefits of starting a community garden include increasing access to healthy, fresh food; providing exercise for people, with a wide range of physical abilities; and creating the opportunity to teach about nutrition, agriculture, and ecology. If you want to get a community garden started, the USDA has a wide variety of resources available to help. There also are plenty of ideas on the Internet and in published materials. Usually, you don't have to have a "green thumb" to garden—just a bit of grit and gumption to get your hands dirty, put seeds or plants in the ground, and then tend to them.

Cornell University's Cooperative Extension Program sponsors a Green Teen Community Gardening Program that helps urban youth learn "life and work skills through hands-on experiences in farming and gardening, health and nutrition, entrepreneurship, and leadership." Throughout the school year, the teens "grow plants and vegetables in their classrooms, on farms, and in community gardens."[16]

Not all community gardens are in urban areas, as Heifer International (HI) has proven. HI is a nonprofit organization that works worldwide to feed the hungry. In rural Cedar Grove, North Carolina, Anathoth Community Garden began in 2005 as an effort to strengthen the community, but those who participated were aging or unable to handle the hard work of gardening. So by 2009, with a grant from Heifer, the community garden manager hired teenagers to work in the garden alongside older folks for one dollar more per hour than minimum wage. The teenagers had committed offenses like shoplifting and illegal drug possession, but the program's goal was to help the teens abandon their lifestyles (which included unhealthy eating practices as well as antisocial behavior) and become involved in organic gardening and helping to feed themselves and others. But several teenagers balked and had no interest in giving up their fast-food diets. As one teen puts it, "I just want my food cheap and plentiful, which is why I support industrial agriculture."[18] Yet, other participants were eager to continue their efforts and proudly showed off the vegetables from their garden, which became ingredients for a homemade pizza.

Notes

1. "Area Youth Groups Gather for Tree Planting in Dorchester," *New England Roots and Shoots*, July 21, 2008, http://nerootsandshoots.blogspot.com/2008/07/area-youth-groups-gather-for-tree.html (accessed August 14, 2011).

2. "Pacific Northwest Research Station: Old Growth—A Unique Ecosystem," *Northwest Research Station*, n.d., www.oregonwild.org/oregon_forests/old_growth_protection/pacific-

northwest-research-station-old-growth-a-unique-ecosystem (accessed June 26, 2011).

3. Kathlyn Gay, ed., *American Dissidents: An Encyclopedia of Activists, Subversives, and Prisoners of Conscience* (Santa Barbara, CA: ABC-CLIO, 2012), pp. 294–298.

4. Kathlyn Gay, *Rainforests of the World*, 2nd edition (Santa Barbara, CA: ABC-CLIO, 2001), p. 8.

5. "Rainforest Facts," *Rain-Tree*, n.d., www.rain-tree.com/facts.htm (accessed June 29, 2011).

6. Julie Jargon, "Cookie Crumbles for Girl Scouts, as Teens Launch Palm-Oil Crusade," *Wall Street Journal*, May 20, 2011, http://online.wsj.com/article/SB10001424052748704281504576327733659636782.html (accessed June 28, 2011).

7. David J. Nowak, et al., *Sustaining America's Urban Trees and Forests* (Washington, DC: U.S. Department of Agriculture, 2010), p. 2.

8. "Andy Lipkis and TreePeople," segment from *It's Easy Being Green*, *DistilleryPictures*, uploaded July 14, 2008, www.youtube.com/watch?v=tMfETbPVy_8 (accessed May 5, 2011).

9. "Three Teenagers Work to Save the Planet," *2 Works for You*, December 16, 2010, www.kjrh.com/dpp/news/problem_solvers/three-teenagers-work-to-save-the-planet (accessed August 14, 2011).

10. Arbor Day Foundation, "Oak Becomes America's National Tree," Press Release, December 10, 2004, www.arborday.org/media/pressreleases/pressrelease.cfm?id=95 (accessed November 8, 2011).

11. "Humboldt Park Teens Grow Gardens to Fight Diabetes," *CBS Chicago*, May 30, 2011, http://chicago.cbslocal.com/2011/05/30/humboldt-park-teens-grow-gardens-to-fight-diabetes (accessed June 30, 2011).

12. "Community Gardens Reap Rewards," *Ohio State University Extension, Urban Programs*, April 30, 2008, http://urbanprograms.osu.edu/urban-impacts/gardening/community-gardens-reap-rewards (accessed July 1, 2011).

13. Federation of Neighborhood Centers, "Teen Testimonials," *Teens 4 Good*, April 28, 2010, http://teens4good.orbius.com/About-Us.page (accessed July 1, 2011).

14. *Philadelphia Orchard Project*, n.d., www.phillyorchards.org/orchards (accessed August 9, 2011).

15. Alison Bryant, "Community Garden Will Give Takoma Park Teens an Opportunity to Blossom," *Gazette.Net*, May 18, 2011, http://ww2.gazette.net/stories/05182011/silvnew205035_32537.php (accessed July 1, 2011).

16. "Green Teen Community Gardening Program," *Cornell University, Cooperative Extension, Dutchess County*, 2011, www.ccedutchess.org/4h/green-teen-community-gardening-program (accessed August 9, 2011).

17. Katie Mintz, "Edina Teens Plant Alley Garden," *Minnesota Sun*, July 20, 2011, www.mnsun.com/articles/2011/07/26/edina/news/ed21mcmgarden.txt (accessed August 9, 2011).

18. Fred Bahnson, "Field of Teens," *Heifer International*, n.d., www.heifer.org/site/c.edJRKQNiFiG/b.7506261 (accessed August 9, 2011).

BUYING GREEN

....

"Conventionally grown fruits and vegetables are often coated with harmful pesticide residues, which generally do not wash off. Organic foods, however, rarely have pesticide residues."—anonymous teenager in an essay for Teen Ink[1]

"**S**ee you at the mall." It's a common way to meet friends, socialize, and shop. If you are intent on buying green—that is, making eco-friendly choices in what you buy—then how do you determine whether clothing, electronics, furniture, shoes, makeup, and so forth are green? The answer is not always easy to find. The same can be said for grocery shopping or buying gardening or building materials, cleaning supplies, carpeting, bedding, and even pet products.

First, it is helpful to remember that every time we make a purchase, we are, in effect, taking action in favor of a specific product. So it is important to know how items are manufactured, what raw materials are used, and how they are packaged, if applicable. One way to find out is to check labels on products. But another big question mark appears: What do the many and varied green labels mean?

Understanding Labels

Perhaps you want to buy a flat-screen television. How do you know if it is eco-friendly? If it has an Energy Star label (the written word *energy* ending with a large star), the television meets strict energy-efficiency guidelines set by the U.S. Environmental Protection Agency (EPA). Televisions that are qualified to attach the Energy Star label use about 40 percent less energy than standard units—that includes even the largest flat-screen plasma TVs. Other products that could qualify for the Energy Star include air conditioners, electronics, and major appliances, such as refrigerators and stoves.

On a wide variety of products, you may find the Green Seal—a large green checkmark on a blue globe. The Green Seal organization declares that it is an "independent non-profit organization dedicated to safeguarding the environment and transforming the marketplace by promoting the manufacture, purchase, and use of environmentally responsible products and services," such as construction materials, paint, food packaging, hand soap, and commercial cleaning services.[2]

When it comes to cleaning products, EPA has a Design for the Environment (DfE) label. That means that the DfE scientific review team has screened each ingredient for potential human health and environmental effects and that the product contains only those ingredients that pose the least concern among chemicals in their class. The EPA says the scientists at EPA have studied chemicals for thirty years or even longer and that the DfE label appears on more than two thousand products.

For green wood and paper products, look for the Forest Stewardship Council (FSC) label—a figure that looks like an evergreen tree with *FSC* below it. The council says on its website that it is an "independent, non-governmental, not-for-profit organization established to promote the responsible management of the world's forests."[3] That means materials come from sustainable forests, not those that have been logged illegally or have abused workers.

The EcoLogo label is a certification established by the Canadian government but recognized worldwide. It "assures that products and services bearing the logo meet stringent standards of environmental leadership."[4]

If you go to a bookstore, chances are you'll find books that were printed on recycled paper with eco-friendly inks. That type of information usually is on the back cover or just inside in the front matter. Other paper products, like notebooks, envelopes, labels, and printer or copy paper, may indicate they are manufactured from recycled materials.

Harry Potter Goes Green

Most Harry Potter fans don't associate their fictional hero with green living, but Scholastic, which partnered with Rainforest Alliance, published the 784-page *Harry Potter and the Deathly Hallows* (2007) on 30-percent recycled paper. Also, the Forest Stewardship Council certified that the "deluxe" edition contained 100-percent recycled paper. When Raincoast Books of Canada published an earlier book, *Harry Potter and the Order of the Phoenix* (2003), the company used 100-percent recycled paper.

Shopping Organic

At many supermarkets today, the organic label is prominent on some fresh and packaged foods, from avocados to processed cereals. Over the past two to three decades, organic foods have become increasingly popular because consumers believe organically grown foods are healthier than crops grown in traditional ways. An anonymous teenager writes in Teen Ink, "Another major reason consumers are buying organic foods is for health concerns. Conventionally grown fruits and vegetables are often coated with harmful pesticide residues, which generally do not wash off. Organic foods, however, rarely have pesticide residues."[5]

As growers and processors began placing organic labels on products that may or may not have adhered to national organic standards, confusion reigned. But the Organic Foods Production Act of 1990 requires the secretary of agriculture to establish a national list of allowed and prohibited substances, which identifies what can and cannot be used in organic production and handling operations.

The U.S. Department of Agriculture (USDA) organic seal is a round label with the words *USDA ORGANIC* inside the circle. It may be printed in green and brown, in black and white, or outlined in black on a transparent background. It may appear on raw or fresh produce or on processed products that contain organic

Is it really organic? Check the label.

agricultural ingredients. Or it may appear on a sign above an organic produce display. On multi-ingredient products, the seal is usually placed on the front of the package, although it may be placed anywhere on the package. When you see this seal, you know the product is at least 95-percent organic.[6]

Some products contain at least 75-percent organic materials, but they are not allowed to use the organic seal. However, the phrase "made with organic ingredients" may be placed on the package. Any processed product with less than 70-percent organic ingredients cannot claim it is organic, although ingredients that are organically produced can be listed on the ingredients statement.

Food products are not the only organics you might buy. How about jeans, T-shirts, hoodies, sweats, and other apparel made of organic cotton? Other organic cotton products include socks, scarves, towels, bathrobes, sheets, blankets, bedding, diapers, and even stationery and notecards. In addition, organic cottonseed is used for animal feed, and organic cottonseed oil is used in a variety of food products, including cookies and chips. According to the Organic Trade Association, "In May 2010, global sales of organic cotton apparel and home textile products reached an estimated $4.3 billion in 2009. This reflects a 35 percent increase from the $3.2 billion market recorded in 2008."[7]

Organic cotton clothing may be more expensive than clothes made from cotton grown the traditional way, but conventionally grown cotton is not eco-friendly. Most cotton grown in the United States requires the use of chemical pesticides because the plants attract many pests, such as the boll weevil and fungi. Reportedly, in the United States, 25 percent of all chemical pesticides used for crop production are used on cotton plants. After the cotton is harvested, pesticides may remain in the soil, which can poison wildlife and seep into water supplies.

Organic farmers, however, eliminate chemical pesticides, fertilizers, fungicides, and defoliants to grow cotton and instead use biological controls. One biological control is the use of pheromones, natural compounds that insects secrete to mark territories or attract mates. Cotton growers may fog fields with a pheromone that disrupts the mating of the bollworm, a pest that destroys cotton plants worldwide.

It Happened to Teen Farmers

Buying organic foods is not what teams of Austin, Texas, teenagers do. Rather, they are farming interns who grow organic vegetables and fruits at a garden site called Urban Roots near the Colorado River. They plant, cultivate, and harvest produce that goes to a food bank to help feed poor families in Austin or to a farmers' market in a low-income urban neighborhood. The teenagers receive a small stipend for working the land, beginning in February when they compost and prepare the soil and later when they plant, weed, and harvest their crops. Mathew, a high school football player, says he appreciates the pay "but I don't think people really care about the money. Hunger is a big problem in Austin, and we get to help with that. That's really what we're here for."

Yet, the teen teams, who gave themselves the nicknames Alpha Dogs, the Beastly Beets, and the Crazy Chickweeds, have learned a lot about organic farming as they grow chives, chard, cucumbers, melon, and other foods and flowers. Nikki is one of the teenagers who loves the urban farm. She notes, "You have to take care of every plant differently. You have to know when their season is, and rotate them so you don't tire out the soil. A lot of weeds will come up if you don't keep up with it," Mathew explains. "We just pull the weeds, we don't use any chemicals. We use fish emulsion for fertilizer, and attractor crops—those are crops that attract the bees so they pollinate, and attract the bugs to keep them from going after the other crops, like tomatoes."[8]

In the United States, products with an organic cotton label must be made from fabric that meets strict federal regulations covering how the cotton is grown. For authentic organic cotton apparel and accessories at reasonable prices, try retailers like Levis, No Sweat, Patagonia, Demockraties, Freedom Clothing, and Maggie's Organics. Their products are featured online.

Some Green Tips for Shopping

Wherever you shop and whatever you buy, the following are some examples of how you can ease the burden on the planet:

- Try thrift shops for clothing, furniture, lamps, utensils, tools, and other items that may be slightly used. You save the energy and packaging that is required for new materials.
- Buy produce at a local farmer's market, thus reducing energy for transporting vegetables and fruits long distances.
- Purchase grains and other nonperishable foods in bulk, which not only saves money but also saves on packaging and fuel needed to transport processed goods to supermarkets.
- Take reusable cloth bags to carry what you buy rather than having your items placed in plastic bags.

Buying Green via Vegetarianism

Some living green advocates turn to vegetarian eating as part of their eco-friendly lifestyle. Elyse May is a teenage vegetarian who declares that she chose that diet because "I love and care for animals." She adds that her teen friends who became vegetarians also did so because they love animals or are concerned about the environment. Others chose vegetarianism because they thought it was a healthy way to eat or because it is "cool." Elyse doesn't think it's a good idea to become a vegetarian "just because it's cool . . . but as long as it saves animals, it's ok with me!" Elyse has coauthored a book, *Veggie Teens: A Cookbook and Guide for Teenage Vegetarians*, available from her website. The book "started as a school project but with a little help from her mom, a family physician, and her dad, a professional chef, it became a mission to help other teenage vegetarians and their families."[9]

Using cloth bags like these is one way to reduce packaging and plastic.

Off the Bookshelf: Green Gone Wrong

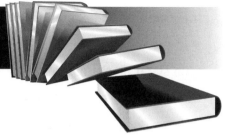

Does buying green really truly help save the earth? Author and journalist Heather Rogers declares it is "lazy environmentalism" in her book *Green Gone Wrong: How Our Economy Is Undermining the Environmental Revolution*. It's not that the author is against shopping with eco-friendly products in mind. Rather it's the fact that "all the billboards, T-shirts, logos, and ads that declare buying this brand at that store will help save the environment can persuade us that it's possible to shop our way out of global warming" and other environmental hazards. She continues, "We would be well served to consider that all those messages of doing right by the planet, and all those eco-products on sale . . . might just be a form of appeasement." Rogers traveled to forests, fields, factories, and corporate headquarters around the world to learn how attempts to be eco-friendly are being undermined (almost sabotaged) by profit-minded industries and political interests. She writes of corporations, for example, that clear-cut forests in developing countries to grow crops for biofuels. Or she describes some USDA inspectors who certify organic produce without ever entering a farmer's field or analyzing soil. These and other practices are obstacles to achieving an eco-friendly world. As Rogers notes, "Shopping green is alluring in part because it is simple (albeit often expensive), unlike the messy business of working toward systemic change" that would include substantive efforts to curb global warming, "sustain holistic farming and food," establish alternative energy sources, and "make major investments in mass transit." She concludes, however, with a positive message in the last chapter, "Notes on the Possible."[10]

Julia of Northfield, Minnesota, became a vegetarian after she saw a video when she was ten years old of what happened to animals at a slaughterhouse. Now as a teenager the very thought of eating meat "makes me feel sick."[11]

Seventeen-year-old Emma also watched a video about animal slaughter. Afterward, she realized these animals feel pain, horror, confusion. You can see it on their faces. Hear it in the sounds. Besides, some of the clips of the way the workers beat or even stand on the animals! . . . I couldn't believe it! And when you stop to think that they take an animal, shock it, slit its throat, strap it by the leg(s) to a conveyor belt and it's carried through the factory and skinned, butchered, eventually packaged . . . the same way they make, like, mustard! It's . . . weird. And to me, wrong. These are real, living, breathing, sensory creatures. I don't understand why some people turn their eyes when a lion kills a gazelle on Animal Planet but then they go and eat a hamburger. We're conscious beings. We can make better choices. We don't need meat to survive.[13]

An estimated 1.4 million teenagers say they are vegetarians. But that may not mean the same thing to all of them because there are several types of vegetarians. Basically, a vegetarian does not eat meat, fish, or fowl or products made with these foods; beyond this, there are a number of diverse eating patterns. A vegan (pronounced *VEE-gun*) eats only plant foods: fruits, vegetables, legumes (such as dried beans and peas), grains, seeds, nuts, and soy products. A lacto-vegetarian eats plant foods plus cheese and other dairy products. Lacto-ovo-vegetarians do not eat meat, fish, or poultry but, along with plant foods, eat eggs, milk, and dairy products like cheese and yogurt. Some people consider themselves semi-vegetarians—they do not eat red meat but include chicken and fish with plant foods, dairy products, and eggs.

Since about the 1960s, animal-rights groups have been spreading their message that nonhuman animals have a right to be free from pain and suffering and that slaughtering animals for food is cruel, unhealthy, and immoral. Some believe that there is no difference between meat eaters and cannibals—both eat meat derived from animals, they contend. In addition, such vegetarians argue that the earth's productive land could grow much more food for humans per acre if grains, vegetables, and other plant foods were raised for human consumption rather than grains only for animal feed.

Anyone wanting to know more about "being veggie" can find information on websites like these:

- *Young Veggies* (www.youngveggie.org)
- *Vegetarian Nutrition for Teenagers* (www.vrg.org/nutrition/teennutrition .htm)
- *Vegetarian Times* (www.vegetariantimes.com)
- *MedlinePlus Vegetarian Diet* (www.nlm.nih.gov/medlineplus/vegetariandiet .html)
- *The Vegetarian Society* (www.vegsoc.org)
- *Girls Health Vegetarian Eating* (www.girlshealth.gov/nutrition/vegetarian/ index.cfm)

Labor Exploitation

Another important factor in buying green is whether workers who manufacture a product or grow and harvest food are being treated fairly and with dignity. After all, sustainability includes consideration of social responsibilities, such as working and living conditions of laborers. Such organizations as Global Exchange, the National Labor Committee, and many university student groups have called attention to apparel and sports shoe companies that exploit workers in the United States and abroad. The workers often labor in sweatshops, a term that describes illegal operations such as ignoring laws governing wages and hours and violating fire and building codes.

Anti-sweatshop campaigns have brought about some reforms, such as corporate codes of conduct that prohibit the use of child labor and recognize workers' right to organize and work in a healthy, safe environment. The code also limits the work week to sixty hours and sets a minimum wage. Companies that abide by the code are certified to use a "no-sweat" label or other type of tag stating that their goods are not manufactured in sweatshops.

Buyer Beware: Greenwashing

While being aware of sustainable practices and attempting to live green, consumers at the same time have to beware of "greenwashing." For centuries, people have used the metaphor of *whitewashing* to indicate a cover-up of a crime or scandal or that something has been painted over (whitewash is a low-cost white paint made from lime) to appear better than it actually is. So it follows that "greenwashing" is also a cover-up. Some companies may advertise that their goods and services are green—eco-friendly—but their claims are misleading, irrelevant, only partially true, or are outright falsehoods. Some examples come from the Federal Trade Commission's (FTC) Bureau of Consumer Protection:

- A box of cereal is labeled "recycled package." The package consists of a paperboard box with a wax paper bag inside holding the cereal. By itself, the claim "recycled package" could apply to both the box and the bag. If only the box is recycled, the claim is deceptive. It should be qualified to say, for example, "recycled box."
- The packaging on a pad of writing paper claims that the writing paper is "environmentally safe because it was not chlorine bleached, a process that has been shown to create harmful substances." Although the paper was not bleached with chlorine, the production process created and released significant quantities of other harmful substances into the environment. The "environmentally safe" claim would be deceptive.
- Environmental seals-of-approval, eco-seals, and certifications from third-party organizations imply that a product is environmentally superior to other products. Because such broad claims are difficult to substantiate, seals-of-approval should be accompanied by information that explains the basis for the award. If the seal-of-approval implies that a third party has certified the product, the certifying party must be truly independent from the advertiser and must have professional expertise in the area that is being certified.
- A paperboard "just add water and eat" soup container is labeled "Please Recycle." Collection sites for this paperboard soup container are not available

to a substantial majority of consumers or communities where the product is sold, making the "Please Recycle" claim deceptive.

- A dealer of used automotive parts recovers a serviceable engine from a vehicle that has been totaled. Without repairing, rebuilding, remanufacturing, or altering the engine or its components in any way, the dealer attaches a "Recycled" label to the engine and offers it for resale in its used auto parts store. Here, the unqualified recycled content claim is not deceptive because consumers are likely to understand that the engine is used and has not been rebuilt.[14]

There are many other examples on the FTC website, and as of 2011, the commission was in the process of revising its guidelines in an attempt to make them more specific. While the FTC does not establish laws regarding green assertions, the commission can and has filed lawsuits against companies for making false environmental claims.

In 2010, Charles Kernaghan, head of the National Labor Committee founded in New York City to combat sweatshops, issued a report, *China's Youth Meet Microsoft*. The report begins with a photograph of young Chinese teenagers asleep at their desks while on a break during a fifteen-hour workday making technology products for Microsoft and other companies, such as Hewlett-Packard and Samsung. Kernaghan states that photographs of workers were "smuggled out of the KYE Systems factory in the south of China." The teenagers shown in the photographs make products like an optical mouse and laser mouse, which are "not necessarily ones the American people would associate with Microsoft. Unfortunately these are Microsoft products, and Microsoft has been outsourcing production to the KYE factory since at least 2003." The young Chinese women who work in the factory live in "primitive" dormitories that house fourteen workers in each room. They sleep on two-level bunk beds and must supply their own mattresses. Each floor of the dormitory has two public bathrooms. To wash up, the young women must "fetch hot water in a small plastic bucket to take a sponge bath." At the factory, the teenagers are "prohibited from talking, listening to music or using the bathroom during working hours." They are also required to stay on the property. Kernaghan's report prompted an investigation by Microsoft and a promise of continual audits of the KYE factory.[14]

Of course, it is not possible for most Americans to individually investigate factories or other facilities overseas that manufacture goods for U.S. consumption. But there could be an opportunity to visit a large U.S. vegetable farm or orchard to see how farmworkers are treated. Or try a day working in the fields, picking lettuce or other crops. Most people quit after a few hours of such work.

Usually migrant workers—immigrants from Mexico or South America—do the hard labor of planting, weeding, and harvesting food. These farmworkers are among the lowest paid in the U.S. labor force—if they get what they are owed. They face many health and safety hazards on the job, often lacking adequate toilets and drinking water. The lack of water caused the death of seventeen-year-old Maria Isabel Vasquez Jimenez in 2008 while she was working in a California vineyard. Her body temperature rose to 108°.

Students, religious groups, sustainable food organizations, and other nonfarm workers across the United States have participated in boycotts and protest marches to publicize conditions of tomato pickers who work in the fields of Immokalee in southwestern Florida. That is where about 90 percent of U.S. tomatoes are grown between October and June.

For decades, the pickers earned $0.40 to $0.45 for every 32-pound (14.5 kg) bucket of tomatoes picked. In 2001 the pickers—members of the Coalition of Immokalee Workers (CIW)—began the Campaign for Fair Food. Through the campaign, news reporters learned of and wrote articles about workers who literally were enslaved by their employers and forced not only to work in the fields but to live in deplorable conditions. With the publicity and the Fair Food Campaign, McDonald's, Burger King, and Yum! Brands (which owns Taco Bell, Pizza Hut, Long John Silver's, and Kentucky Fried Chicken) agreed to pay at least one cent more per pound for the tomatoes they purchased. As of mid-2011, other giant chains, such as Stop and Shop, Kroger, Trader Joe's, and Publix, have refused to negotiate for the one-cent increase, insisting that the CIW should address the people who hire tomato pickers, not food retailers and their customers.

Notes

1. "Organic Foods: Are They Worth the Price?" *Teen Ink*, July 2010, www.teenink.com/hot_topics/environment/article/4355/Organic-Foods-Are-they-worth-the-price (accessed July 18, 2011).
2. "Frequently Asked Questions," *Green Seal*, 2011, www.greenseal.org/AboutGreenSeal/FrequentlyAskedQuestions.aspx (accessed July 17, 2011).
3. "About FSC," *Forest Stewardship Council*, n.d., www.fsc.org/about-fsc.html (accessed July 18, 2011).
4. "About EcoLogo," *EcoLogo Program*, n.d., www.ecologo.org/en (accessed August 9, 2011).
5. "Organic Foods: Are They Worth the Price?" *Teen Ink*, July 2010, www.teenink.com/hot_topics/environment/article/4355/Organic-Foods-Are-they-worth-the-price (accessed July 18, 2011).
6. "Organic Labeling and Marketing Information," *U.S. Department of Agriculture, Agricultural Marketing Service*, April 2008, www.ams.usda.gov/AMSv1.0/getfile?dDocName=STELDEV3004446 (accessed July 18, 2011).
7. "Organic Cotton Facts," *Organic Trade Association*, June 2010, www.ota.com/organic/mt/organic_cotton.html (accessed July 20, 2011).
8. Abe Louise Young, "Urban Teenagers Grow 25,000 Pounds of Organic Produce to Relieve Hunger," *What Kids Can Do*, July 2010, www.whatkidscando.org/featurestories/2010/07_urban_teenagers/index.html (accessed July 18, 2011).
9. *Veggie Teens: A Cookbook and Guide for Vegetarian Teenagers*, n.d., www.veggieteenscookbook.com/teenagers (accessed July 20, 2011).
10. Heather Rogers, *Green Gone Wrong: How Our Economy Is Undermining the Environmental Revolution* (New York: Simon & Schuster, 2010), p. 186.
11. Joni Berg, "Teen Vegetarians Keeping It Healthy," *Northfield News*, June 7, 2011, www.northfieldnews.com/content/teen-vegetarians-keeping-it-healthy (accessed July 20, 2011).
12. "Why I Went Veggie," *Young Veggie*, n.d., www.youngveggie.org/being_veggie/why_I_went_veggie.html (accessed July 21, 2011).
13. "Complying with the Environmental Marketing Guides," *Federal Trade Commission Bureau of Consumer Protection*, May 2000, http://business.ftc.gov/documents/bus42-complying-environmental-marketing-guides (accessed April 30, 2011).
14. Charles Kernaghan, *China's Youth Meet Microsoft* (New York: National Labor Committee, April 2010), www.nlcnet.org/admin/reports/files/Chinas_Youth_Meet_Micro.pdf (accessed December 4, 2010).

REDUCING, REUSING, RECYCLING

··

"My school was really, really nit-picky about where you put your leftovers from food. They'd make sure there was nothing in the trash can that couldn't be composted or recycled."—Meagan Traylor, a student at New Vista High School in Boulder, Colorado[1]

While recycling and reusing are important aspects of living green, reducing consumption can be even more significant. In fact the slogan "reduce, reuse, recycle" suggests that reduction should be at the top of the list. In other words, the need to recycle and find ways to reuse products could be lowered if we purchased less "stuff." That, however, is not a message advertisers, manufacturers, marketers, and other sellers want to impart. Consumerism is supposed to keep the U.S. economy functioning and provide jobs. Yet, the more we consume, the more we seem to throw away: clothes, electronics, furniture, toys, small appliances, sports equipment, tools, and many other items. In fact, America has become known as the throwaway society, and waste of all types piles up.

The Environmental Protection Agency (EPA) says, "The most effective way to reduce waste is to not create it in the first place. . . . Unfortunately, the amount of waste generated in the United States has been increasing. Between 1960 and 2009 the amount of waste each person creates increased from 2.7 to 4.3 pounds per day. This results in about 243 million tons of waste generated in the US in 2009."[2]

Food leftovers are a major source of waste. According to a study by the U.S. Department of Agriculture (USDA), Americans waste 96 billion pounds (43.5 billion kg) of food each year. That breaks down to more than 263 million pounds

(119 million kg) of wasted food each day and almost 11 million pounds (5 million kg) each hour. According to *Live Science*, a "'staggering' amount of food is tossed out as garbage. . . . In the United States, as much as 30 percent of food, worth about $48.3 billion, is tossed out each year."[3] Much of that food garbage could be composted, used to generate fuel, or recycled in some other manner.

Supermarkets throw out much food—especially produce, meats, poultry, and seafood—because of spoilage. Marketing also plays a role in food waste: consumers may buy more than they need or can use with promotions like "buy one, get one free."

School cafeterias are another source of food waste, although many schools are changing that situation. Many colleges and high schools have cut cafeteria waste and reduced consumption by serving food on dinner plates rather than trays. Because plates hold less than trays, students are less likely to pile up food that may not be eaten. Thus they throw less away.

Reducing consumption, as many who live green already know, is a matter of thinking twice (or three or four times) about our use of products and services in our "culture of consumerism," as it has been called. As some individuals and groups have pointed out, they are attempting to reduce their carbon footprints, use less energy and fuel, decrease water consumption, buy less (or only what they need), repair what they can rather than buy new products, and share what they have learned about eco-friendly living.

Jenn Oliver, an environmental management student at Penn State University (University Park) puts it this way: "I've learned that big results can come from making small lifestyle changes. . . . I try to share this information with everyone that I know and the students I meet."[4]

Reusing

Glass jars can be reused for food storage, and they are excellent containers for nuts and bolts and other small items. Many other common objects can be reused. Consider plastic bags. Although they can be recycled, they can be reused to line small trash containers in the kitchen, bathroom, bedroom, or in the car. Small plastic containers can become garden traps by filling them with beer and placing them in the garden to lure slugs and other pests.

Some schools and communities conduct drives to collect old sneakers for Nike's Reuse-a-Shoe program. After shoes are collected, they go to a Nike recycling center, where each shoe is cut into three slices—rubber outsole, foam midsole, and fiber upper. The outsole is ground up to make materials for track and playground surfaces and gym floor tiles. Foam insoles are reused to produce cushioning materials for outdoor basketball and tennis courts. Shoe fiber is reused to make cushioning for indoor courts. Nike claims that each year more than 1.5 million shoes are collected worldwide for reuse.[6]

> **It's a Fact**
>
> *Mindfully.org*, an organization providing information on a wide variety of environmental issues, says, "Reducing consumption without reducing use is a costly delusion. If undeveloped countries consumed at the same rate as the U.S., four complete planets the size of the Earth would be required. People who think that they have a right to such a life are quite mistaken."[5]

For green living, here are some more ideas:

- Donate reusables to homeless shelters or charities.
- Buy things you need from a thrift shop, such as furniture or drapes for a dorm room.
- Create small blankets or quilts for nursery schools by sewing together pieces of scrap cloth.
- Request heavy-duty cardboard boxes from grocery stores to reuse for storage or shipping.
- Reuse chipped coffee mugs as pencil and pen holders.
- Give used books to the Veterans Administration, public library, homeless shelter, or another charity.

Reusing Plastic Bottles

Make a mini greenhouse out of plastic bottles. That's what *Green Living Tips and Ideas* suggests and explains that "mini greenhouses can be used to start cuttings, protect an ailing plant, or to start seeds." How? The website has these instructions:

First, you will have to find a bottle that fits over the container you want to enclose in a greenhouse environment. Cut the bottom off of the bottle with sharp scissors or a razor knife. Then, simply invert the bottle over your cutting. Your soil should be moist, but not wet. You should be able to see through your plastic bottle at all times. If your bottle clouds up to a point where you can't see what's inside, you should remove the bottle and let the soil dry out a little before replacing it.[7]

Hair Today, Gone Tomorrow

Call it recyclable, reusable, and renewable—all the adjectives apply to hair—human hair. Hair is used to make hair booms and hair mats. Hair is stuffed into recycled panty hose to absorb oil spills on waterways and beaches. An organization that specializes in that process is Matter of Trust. It collects hair clippings from barber shops and salons. Phil McCrory, an Alabama hair stylist, came up with the idea for a hair mat. McCrory had watched TV programs picturing the Exxon Valdez oil spill in 1989, and he noticed how the fur on Alaskan otters became saturated with oil. He began to test how much oil could be absorbed with hair clippings from his salon. From that experiment came the hair mat. In the United States, 370,000 salons each cut about a pound of hair per day. That adds up to an estimated 135 million pounds each year, a huge renewable resource that can be recycled and reused.

This is a familiar recycling loop symbol, and recycling is one of the most common green activities.

While some recycled hair helps the environment, locks of hair, such as ponytails and braids, can be cut and used to create wigs for people who lose their hair as a result of chemotherapy treatments for cancer or an autoimmune disease called alopecia areata or who suffer from aplastic anemia, a blood disorder. Locks of Love (www.locksoflove.org) provides wigs for people under the age of twenty-one, and Wigs for Kids (www.wigsforkids.org) is another program that creates wigs for disadvantaged children with hair loss. Hair that is donated has to be at least ten inches long to be used for a wig (shorter lengths are used to offset costs) and must be clean and dry. Permed and bleached hair is not acceptable; dyed hair is usable. The hair should be shaped into a ponytail or braid that is secured tightly, placed in a plastic bag or wrapped in tissue paper, and mailed to one of the programs named or any other of your choice.

In September 2010, dozens of students at the University of Washington in Seattle took part in an event to cut their hair for Locks of Love. Student Rachel Hart notes, "It's a great way to give back to the community. . . . There are kids out there who need wigs, and if you don't donate, who will?"[8] Similar events take place in many states, and often a salon will help with the cutting and collecting.

Another way hair is reused is as an organic fertilizer—human hair contains nitrogen and amino acids that help plants grow. Hair clippings can enrich soil, as McCrory discovered. He designed a mat called Smart Grow that allows air and moisture to move through the hair and helps it biodegrade and release nutrients. It also absorbs water and controls weeds.

Paper Recycling

According to the EPA, paper makes up 28 percent of municipal solid waste, more than any other material Americans throw away. But when just one ton of paper is recycled, enough energy is saved to power the average American home for six months. In addition, each ton of recycled paper saves seven thousand gallons of water and reduces greenhouse gas emissions.

Recycling clubs are popular in high schools across the United States, and paper recycling has been a major effort at Purdy High School in southwest Missouri since 2005. At the time there was no recycling program in the town. The school's Spanish Club initiated the Purdy Recycling Project as a community service program and as a way to raise funds for the club. Students from the fifth through twelfth grades receive environmental education and are trained to pass on their knowledge about the importance of recycling to their families. By 2008, the all-volunteer program had established a recycling collection and processing center, and in 2010, they recovered twenty-six tons of paper. In addition, they now take in twelve different recoverables.

At Franklin Central High School in Indianapolis, the recycling club's emphasis is on paper recycling. Waste paper is sent to collection centers for recycling into new paper products rather than being thrown out as trash. Shana Cameron, a student at Franklin Central, notes, "I hate how much trash we have."[9]

Many schools are taking advantage of the GreenFiber Community Recycling program. GreenFiber accepts and pays for a wide variety of paper products— brown paper bags, cardboard, cereal boxes, construction paper, gift wrap, magazines, newspaper, paper, and phone books. The company makes natural-fiber blow-in insulation for homes, hospitals, and commercial buildings. With headquarters in Charlotte, North Carolina, GreenFiber has manufacturing plants in diverse areas of the United States, from Albany, New York, to Tampa, Florida, and Salt Lake City, Utah, to Waco, Texas. GreenFiber uses materials that are available locally, placing large green bins on school campuses and outside libraries, fire stations, and businesses. When schools participate in the GreenFiber program, they receive 100 percent of the revenue from all paper products that are recycled. For example, Pasco County (Florida) schools received $48,000 for the assorted paper products—2,211 tons—collected in the 2010 school year.

Paper recycling also takes place in businesses and industries and through curbside pickups of newspapers. Americans use 85 million tons of paper annually, about 680 pounds per person, and the average household throws away 13,000 separate pieces of paper each year. Most is packaging and junk mail, according to *A Recycling Revolution* (recycling-revolution.com).

Many Recyclable Goods

Along with paper a great variety of goods can be recycled, including batteries, cell phones, computers, printers, and other electronics. That was evident at Indiana

Papermaking

Papermaking has a long history, beginning about 105 A.D. in China, although even before that ancient people used a variety of writing materials, such as papyrus and bamboo strips. In America, about three hundred years ago, papermaking began as a recycling industry. Until 1860, paper was made from cloth—linen and cotton rags—as well as some waste paper. With the increasing demand for paper over the next century and with new technology for using wood fibers, mills phased out their use of rags. Many mills used wood pulp as well as recovered fiber from recycled paper.

Environmentalists long have been critical of papermaking from wood pulp because it depletes forests and destroys sinks or holding places for carbon dioxide, one of the gases contributing to global warming. However, as an increasing amount of paper is being recovered and recycled, it is being used in papermaking. In 2010 more than 63 percent of the paper consumed in the United States was recovered for recycling, according to *paperrecycles.org*. That amounts to 334 pounds per person. As a result, more paper was recycled than went to landfills.

Papermaking from recycled material begins with shredding and mixing the recovered fiber with water to form a slurry, or pulp. That pulp is washed to filter out nonfibrous materials, such as glass, metal, plastic, and dirt. Layers of pulp over screens drain away excess water, and huge rollers press out remaining water. Heated rollers dry and sterilize the paper sheets. Finished paper goes to fabricators, who make newsprint, writing and printing paper, brown paper sacks, toilet and facial tissues, paper towels, and napkins. Buying and using these types of recycled paper products is one way of closing the recycling loop.

University, South Bend, during the annual E-waste Recycling Fest in 2011. The *South Bend Tribune* reports, "Stacks of old computers, printers, copy machines, TVs, and other broken or outdated appliances [were] piled high" in the university's parking lot.[10] Tens of thousands of pounds of goods were collected, and Apple,

Inc., provided trucks and workers who carried off truckload after truckload of electronics, whose parts will be recycled.

Teenage twins Jillian and Allison Samowitz of Golden Beach, Florida, came up with an idea for recycling in their city. In 2010, with the help of their parents, they initiated a nonprofit organization called Proseed2Green E-vent, which stressed recycling and saving energy. Although Golden Beach had a recycling program, it was not widely supported. The twins visited businesses and residents to urge recycling. Allison explains, "We're not asking for residents to take extreme measures." Jillian adds, "Small habits make a big impact."[11]

Matt Mooney of Land O' Lakes High School in Pasco County, Florida, has been collecting cans for recycling since 2006, when he decided he wanted to do something to help the environment and also Habitat for Humanity, the volunteer organization that builds affordable houses for people needing help. At the time, Mooney was only thirteen years old and too young to work on construction, but he learned the organization collected aluminum cans for recycling, thus earning funds for building materials. Mooney sought the help from his and other schools, churches, businesses, law enforcement, and construction workers. He had collected more than one million cans by 2009. That year, then-governor Charlie Crist awarded Mooney and the Pasco County School District the Green School Award for their recycling and energy reduction programs. Mooney gave part of his prize of $1,500 to Habitat for Humanity and saved some of the money for college.

If you live in a town or city with a recycling program, handlers may pick up certain recyclables, such as plastic, glass, aluminum cans, and newspapers left in a bin or bag at the street curb, but you may have to call the local waste collector to find out what will be picked up. Some types of plastic containers may not be allowed. Usually the only acceptable glass throwaways are bottles. Glass vases, drinking glasses, mirrors, and the like are not recycled. In some communities, newspapers must be taken to special dumpsters located at schools, religious institutions, or other sites. The same is true for old telephone books and other recyclables, such as tires and motor oil.

Recycling Scrap Tires and Used Motor Oil

When recycling comes to mind, most people don't think about scrap tires or used motor oil. Often scrap tire recycling begins at an automotive repair shop or tire store. Millions of old tires are scrapped each year. They may be dumped illegally in fields, into waterways, or in landfills. Scrap tires above ground collect water, are breeding places for mosquitoes, and attract rodents. When they pile up, tires, which are combustible, become fire hazards.

Nearly all states have regulations regarding disposal of scrap tires, which differ from used tires that may be retreaded and sold. States regulate how scrap tires are collected, stored, and hauled by a transporter to a scrap tire facility or an authorized landfill. When scrap tires are recycled, they may be pulverized and used to manufacture floor mats, asphalt for highways, or other rubberized products. They also may be reused for numerous purposes, such as bumpers for boat and truck docks, planters, raised garden beds, building materials for playground structures, backyard tire swings, and to control soil erosion along banks of waterways.

Recycling used motor oil frequently is a job that vehicle repair shops and garages handle. Do-it-yourselfers can take drained oil to a collection center, where the oil will go from there to a refinery to produce lubricating oil or to a facility that processes the oil for use in furnaces and electric power plants. The American Petroleum Institute says that "if you recycle just two gallons of used oil it can generate enough electricity to run the average household for almost 24 hours."[12]

Scrap Metal Dealers—Major Recyclers

Scrap metal has been recycled for centuries. During wars, farmers in times past often converted their farm implements into swords and spears. Armies tore down metal statues and ornaments, melting them down to form armor and weapons. American colonists collected their copper and iron pots and metal utensils and dropped them in the town square for recycling into weapons to fight the Revolutionary War.

During the Industrial Revolution, immigrant peddlers of the late 1800s and early 1900s collected rags (for papermaking) and old iron for recycling. Their cries echoed in the streets of eastern cities, running their words together in a chant "Any rags-a-lyin' today?" Many of these peddlers began scrap metal yards, collecting large amounts of scrap and processing it for resale and reuse in mills.

Contrary to popular belief, a scrap metal yard is not a junkyard. In fact a junkyard is a salvage yard—parts from wrecked, stolen, or outdated vehicles, for example, may be retrieved and sold. The junk cars may then be sent to a scrap yard, which is like a metal mine above ground. It is a place where scrap material is processed for recycling into new manufactured items, which may again be recycled when scrapped. Recycling scrap metal is big business in the United States, currently generating $85 billion annually.

When scrap metals come into a dealer's yard, they must be sorted into ferrous and nonferrous metals. Iron and steel are ferrous metals, while nonferrous scrap includes aluminum, copper, and lead. Ferrous scrap is by far the largest amount of material processed by a scrap yard, and much of it comes from manufacturing and steel plant leftovers.

Huge machines smash, pound, slice, shred, and bale everything from automobile hulks to steel girders from demolished buildings. For example, if a car ends up in a scrap yard, tires, seats, window glass, batteries, radiators, and most other parts are removed. A crane then picks up the hulk and drops it into the bin of a hydraulic press or baler. With thousands of pounds of pressure, the baler squeezes the car hulk into a compact bundle about the size of a large TV set. Steel scrap is essential for manufacturing steel. In the past nearly all steel making required iron ore mined and shipped to mills, where it was melted down with coal, limestone, and scrap metal. Now furnaces use 100-percent scrap steel.

Aluminum is a major nonferrous metal that is recycled. There is no limit to the number of times it can be recycled. Along with aluminum cans, discarded

These bundles of scrap metal are ready for recycling.

aluminum lawn chair frames, siding and gutters from buildings, and aluminum scrap from industries are processed in a scrap yard. Aluminum must be crushed and bundled or shredded before it can be shipped to a smelting plant, where it will be melted down to produce new aluminum.

Plastic Recycling

Plastic. It seems to be everywhere. Plastic water bottles, jugs, storage containers, dishes, utensils, glasses, toothbrushes, packaging, medication bottles, straws, egg cartons, toys, food trays—the list goes on and on. Plastics have been around since the early 1900s but developed rapidly during World War II, when they were substitutes for scarce materials, especially metals. The strength, versatility, and light weight of plastic materials made them ideal for the military and later for consumer products. Today plastics are so much a part of U.S. life that most of us

It Happened to Marlon

Teenager Marlon Tapang of Gurnee, Illinois, north of Chicago, knows something about scrap metal—that it is recyclable and valuable. Unfortunately, he was the likely victim of scrap metal thieves in May 2011. Someone stole his expensive motorized wheelchair from the driveway of his home. Marlon has cerebral palsy and his chair allowed him to get around without a lot of help. Marlon's father Paul had put the wheelchair outside so it would be ready when the school bus arrived.

Paul went back into the house to help his son get to the bus. When Paul noticed the chair was gone, he assumed the bus driver had loaded it. But when Marlon got to Warren Township High School, his chair was not aboard the bus. Police have no clues but suspect a scrap metal thief stole the chair. These thieves often cruise neighborhoods on garbage collection days; the wheelchair disappeared on such a day.

The Tapang family is not the only victim in their area. Friends reported a thief grabbed their lawn mower and ran off with it even as they tried to catch him.

Across the United States, thieves are stealing objects made of metal that can be sold to a scrap metal dealer for recycling. Some scrap has high value, and thieves grab metal materials from construction sites, vacant homes, and even cemeteries. The U.S. Department of Energy estimates that losses from copper theft alone cost the U.S. economy about $1 billion a year.

A church under construction in Provo, Utah, lost $290,000 worth of metal to a thief. Reportedly "splice plates, base plates, I-beams and other items were taken."[13] Vacant homes are inviting to thieves, who take copper from air conditioners or pull out the entire units to take to recyclers. Thieves have stolen bronze vases from cemeteries, a radio water tower in Pennsylvania, a thousand-pound tractor trailer engine in Ohio, and storm grates and manhole covers in numerous cities.

What was the outcome for Marlon Tapang? Great Lakes Adaptive Sports Association of Lake Forest, which provides equipment for disabled children involved in sports, loaned Marlon a wheelchair. Insurance likely will cover the cost of a new one.[14]

cannot imagine living without them. However, as plastic products have continued to multiply and have become environmental hazards, like the Great Pacific Garbage Patch, what does a person living green try to do? Live without plastic? Some have tried that in vain. So the next best alternative is to reduce the use of plastic materials and recycle as much as you can.

Yet, there are those who do not want to make the effort to recycle. As Shana, the student at Franklin Central High School in Indianapolis points out, her family drinks a lot of milk, but her parents do not want to take the empty plastic jugs to a recycling center. So, she explains, "I throw them in the trunk of my car, and . . . I drive to Kroger, which is right by my house, and they have the big recycling bins over there."[15]

Reducing plastic use may consist of such actions as carrying reusable drinking bottles or cups, wrapping sandwiches in wax paper rather than plastic, eliminating disposable dishes and cutlery and instead substituting reusable dinnerware, and taking cloth bags to stores rather than having purchases put into plastic bags. Empty glass jars (pickle jars, for example) can be reused to hold leftovers in the refrigerator rather than plastic containers. There are lots of ideas for reducing plastic on *My Plastic-free Life* (myplasticfreelife.com), a blog by Beth Terry of California.

Plastic recycling takes place in many communities usually through curbside recycling or at drop-off sites. What happens to the plastics after they are picked up? The EPA says,

> They go to a material recovery facility, where . . . the mixed plastics are sorted by plastic type, baled, and sent to a reclaiming facility. At the facility, any trash or dirt is sorted out, then the plastic is washed and ground into small flakes. A flotation tank then further separates contaminants, based on their different densities. Flakes are then dried, melted, filtered, and formed into pellets. The pellets are shipped to product manufacturing plants, where they are made into new plastic products.[16]

Did You Know?

Curbside recycling programs did not exist in the United States in 1973, but by 2006, about 8,660 curbside programs had sprouted up across the nation, according to the Natural Resources Defense Council. Nevertheless, only 31 percent of plastic soft drink bottles and 45 percent of aluminum cans are now recycled.

Because plastic goods are made from different types of resins, all of them are not recycled in the same way. But plastics are coded to show their type and provide a clue about their recyclability.

The code is a triangle symbol that has a resin identification number, ranging from 1 to 7, inside. However, just because a plastic product has the resin number in a triangle, which looks very similar to the recycling symbol, that does not mean it will be collected for recycling. Number 1 plastic stands for PET or PETE (polyethylene terephthalate) and is found on water and soda bottles; number 2 is HDPE (high-density polyethylene) and is found on containers like milk jugs, juice bottles, bleach jugs, and detergent and shampoo bottles. Both 1 and 2 plastics are readily recyclable. PET bottles are recycled primarily for carpet fibers and textiles, and HDPE containers are recycled to manufacture bottles.

Number 3 stands for vinyl or PVC, which contains chlorine and seldom is recycled, although some manufacturers of plastic lumber may use it to make decks, flooring, and speed bumps. LDPE (low-density polyethylene) is the number 4 resin used for such items as shopping bags, squeezable bottles, and some furniture. Most curbside recycling programs prefer not to pick up LDPE items. Number 5 is PP (polypropylene), and number 6 is PS (polystyrene), from which disposable cups and plates are made. Both 5 and 6 are recyclable. The final code, number 7, stands for miscellaneous plastics that do not fit other categories and may not be easily recycled.

Notes

1. Marisa McNatt, "Teens Say Environment Is a Top Concern," *Earth911.com*, February 2, 2010, http://earth911.com/news/2010/02/25/teens-say-environment-is-a-top-concern (accessed July 26, 2011).

2. U.S. Environmental Protection Agency, "Reduce and Reuse," *Wastes—Resource Conservation—Reduce, Reuse, Recycle*, July 26, 2011, www.epa.gov/osw/conserve/rrr/reduce.htm (accessed July 26, 2011).

3. "Staggering Amount of Food Wasted," *Live Science*, May 14, 2008, www.livescience.com/health/080514-food-wasted.html (accessed April 18, 2009).

4. "Student Story: ERM Student Dedicated to Reducing Consumption," *Penn State Live*, May 19, 2009, http://live.psu.edu/story/39866 (accessed July 28, 2011).

5. "Consumption by the United States," *Mindfully.org*, n.d., www.mindfully.org/Sustainability/Americans-Consume-24percent.htm (accessed August 6, 2011).

6. "Frequently Asked Questions," *Reuse-a-Shoe*, 2008, www.nikereuseashoe.com/faqs (accessed July 29, 2011).

7. "Recycling Plastic Bottles for Mini Greenhouse," *Green Living Tips and Ideas*, July 26, 2010, www.getgreenliving.com/recycling-plastic-bottles-into-mini-greenhouses-and-planting-pots/#comment-2730 (accessed August 13, 2011).

8. Nick Visser, "A Cut for a Cause," *The Daily of the University of Washington*, September 29, 2010, http://dailyuw.com/news/2010/sep/29/a-cut-for-a-cause (accessed July 26, 2011).

9. Quoted in David Glass, Victoria Kreyden, and Izaak Hayes, "Teens Are Committed to Recycling," *Ypress*, June 6, 2009, www.ypress.org/news/teens_are_committed_to_recycling (accessed November 8, 2011).

10. Margaret Fosmoe, "E-waste Stacking Up at Indiana University South Bend," *South Bend Tribune*, May 13, 2011, www.iusb.edu/~csfuture/E-waste%20stacking%20up%20at%20Indiana%20University%20South%20Bend%20-%20southbendtribune.pdf (accessed October 23, 2011).

11. Amelia Gonzalez, "Golden Beach Teens Preach Pluses of Going Green," *Miami Herald*, March 24, 2011, www.miamiherald.com/2011/03/20/2119975/golden-beach-teens-teach-towns.html (accessed July 23, 2011).

12. "Used Motor Oil Collection and Recycling," *American Petroleum Institute*, n.d., www.recycleoil.org/more.html (accessed July 23, 2011).

13. Jim Dalrymple, "Thieves Steal Small Fortune in Scrap Metal from Church," *Daily Herald*, July 1, 2011, www.heraldextra.com/news/local/crime-and-courts/article_0c7121f9-b1e5-53a5-8faf-ba1e4ecd80f6.html (accessed July 24, 2011).

14. Frank Abderholden, "Scrap Metal Thieves May Have Snatched Wheelchair," *News-Sun*, July 3, 2011, http://newssun.suntimes.com/news/5591945-418/scrap-metal-thieves-may-have-snatched-wheelchair.html (accessed July 25, 2011).

15. David Glass, "Teens Are Committed to Recycling," *Ypress: Youth News Network*, June 6, 2009, www.ypress.org/news/teens_are_committed_to_recycling (accessed July 23, 2011).

16. U.S. Environmental Protection Agency, "Wastes—Resource Conservation—Common Wastes and Materials," January 25, 2011, www.epa.gov/osw/conserve/materials/plastics.htm (accessed July 24, 2011).

PARTICIPATING IN GREEN PROJECTS AT SCHOOLS

*"I learned a lot of different things about plants and animals, a lot about vernal pools and
how to build bog bridges, and not only about many types of tools but how to use them."*
—*Massachusetts teenager Brittany Gentilucci, who took younger
students on nature walks as part of a green schools project*[1]

There is no shortage of green project ideas for schools, and in recent years many
U.S. schools have been implementing green programs ranging from collecting
old sneakers for reuse to constructing green buildings on school campuses. A
common school project is marking storm drains. Students use a stencil and paint
such words as "Dump No Waste—Drains to Streams" or "No Dumping—
Drains to River" or "Dump No Waste—Drains to River" to warn residents that
drains are for rainwater only. Students hope to discourage people from dumping
chemicals, paints, pesticides, motor oil, and other hazardous materials into drains.
Such waste, when dumped into drains, goes directly into streams or groundwater,
contaminating these water resources.

A Variety of Green School Projects

In Washington State, the King County Green Schools Program gives an award to
students for their green efforts, and winners are known as "Earth Heroes at School."
Students Cora and Audrey in Woodinville won the award in 2009 for creating a

Green Spirit Week, which highlighted a different environmental issue each day. Each issue was associated with a particular color. For example, Wednesday was the day to wear black as a reminder to turn off lights and electronics, while on Thursday students wore white to encourage reduced paper use. The week culminated with a lunchtime event that reinforced the week's messages.[2]

Issaquah High School student Kate Brunette was one award winner in 2011. Her school's recycling rate was low, so Kate "gathered support from the City of Issaquah, King County Green Schools Program, students, custodial staff, teachers and administration to implement strategies to increase recycling, including adding food scrap collection to the program." Another winner, Cort Hammond of Tahoma High School, also established a recycling program that reduces waste and saves money for the school district. In addition, Cort has done habitat restoration, trail restoration, native planting, and Adopt-a-Road events. The third 2011 winner was Annapurni Sriram of Snoqualmie, who wrote to the town mayor, "urging him to address sustainability and climate change. The mayor invited her to serve on the city's Sustainability Advisory Team."[3]

At the University of Central Florida in Orlando, a school project involves reducing the use of plastic bags by creating tote bags out of old T-shirts; they cut off the shirt's sleeves and neck and sew up the bottom. Another effort is conducting student tours, taking students through campus green space with its natural native landscape and explaining how a species works with other species to thrive and stay alive, according to two members of the project, Henry and Samantha.[4]

More than thirty students at City Academy in Salt Lake City, Utah, have conducted green school projects for at least eight years. One that began in 2003 was making biodiesel from used vegetable oil. Tom, an academy student, reports, "Every year since we have continued to make biodiesel, and to use what we make in the small school bus we obtained for this purpose. The best part is being able to use the City Academy Bio-Diesel Bus for a field trip without consuming fossil

Many students use the Internet at school or at home or at an Internet café like this one to find ideas for green school projects.

fuels. Also, our chemistry class uses making bio-diesel as a form of experiential learning about chemical reactions and their usefulness." He explains that the group "used the Internet to find our small school bus, and to learn more about making bio-diesel from used vegetable oil. We also used the Internet to help us find parts to build our bio-diesel processing equipment."[5]

Other green projects at the academy have included a school garden and a temporary greenhouse to grow plants from seeds. The greenhouse has to be taken down at the end of the school year and then reinstalled at the start of the following school year.

A dozen members of the environmental club at the Milburn (New Jersey) Senior High School initiated a school project that involved collecting plastic water bottles that students had thrown in recycling bins or in the trash. Once they had collected about four hundred of the bottles, they began to assemble their own recycling bin. As Emily, president of the club, explains,

> Using the tops of recycling bins as a base, we used hot glue guns to glue together water bottles into rings. Then, we glued the rings on top of one another to form the shape of a recycling bin. We made two of these and placed them in central parts of our school with recycling posters on them. We also made an announcement during the morning . . . to draw attention to the bins and to share some facts about recycling. The best part was seeing how many water bottles were recycled in the bins. This proved that our project caused more people to recycle.[6]

The Keep Austin Beautiful program in Austin, Texas, involves Green Teens from Eastside Memorial, Lyndon B. Johnson (LBJ), Reagan, and Travis High Schools and also students from two middle schools. LBJ Green Teens' thirteen members garden, pick up trash, build birdfeeders, make wilderness survival kits, and learn about aquifers as well as other environmental topics. During the 2010–2011 school year, LBJ Green Teens cleaned their neighborhood, recruiting friends and family members along the way to help. Most were distressed by the amount of trash they found. At Reagan High School in Austin a group of Green Teens adopted a community garden plot, watering and checking on their seedlings multiple times a week and feeding the pet chicken. While attending community garden meetings, Green Teens found that gardening has career possibilities and is a great way to meet community members. Travis High Green Teens explored a nearby nature preserve to identify native and invasive plants and to pick up trash wherever they discovered it. While on a routine hike, students spotted a red-tail hawk and watched its activity through the class period, which heightened student awareness of all the preserve has to offer. Eastside Memorial students created a courtyard garden, including a vegetable plot, at their school.[7]

At Olathe South High School in Olathe, Kansas, students Ian Lally, Katie Blackmon, Leah Darlington, and Tyler Meeks initiated a carpool plan to reduce carbon footprints. The plan includes the following:

- By having students carpool they will be rewarded with premium parking that only carpool participants will receive. When enacted, students can choose to sign up in the office with forms provided to them that we have created. Student's and parent's signatures are required to participate in this activity.

- When students turn in their form they will also have to give up their regular Olathe South parking pass before they receive their "Carpool Pass." One pass will be given per group and the pass must be hung in the carpooling car at all times. If a student's partner is not attending school that day they must park in the regular parking locations. Carpooling spots will be marked off with green paint and green blockades, and these spots are the premium spots because they are closest to the doors. The carpool parking permits will be green and say "Olathe South Carpool" and participants will not have to pay anything for this pass.[8]

The nonprofit organization Alliance to Save Energy (ASE) has a Green Schools Program that was initiated in 1996 to help schools save on energy costs and to provide opportunities for students to be advocates for the environment. Students in the program learn about the importance of energy efficiency and are trained to assess the energy usage in their school. According to ASE, "Through basic changes in operations, maintenance and individual behavior, schools participating in the Green Schools Program have achieved reductions in energy use of 5 to 15

It Happened to the Teens Turning Green (TTG) Organization

It all started with a Marin County, California, student, Erin Schrode, who has been campaigning for and buying green products for years. In 2005, Schrode, a sometimes model, and her mother, Judi Shils, a former TV producer and environmental activist, initiated a program called Teens for Safe Cosmetics. The program began with teenagers meeting at Schrode's home and learning about poisonous ingredients in cosmetics, toxins that are linked to cancer and other deadly diseases. Schrode and other teens lobbied the California legislature to pass a bill that would require manufacturers of body-care products and cosmetics to label cancer-causing and reproductive-toxicity ingredients. The California Safe Cosmetics Act passed in October 2005.

By 2007, the teens had branched out and become TTG, with chapters in schools and student organization across the United States. As a student-led movement, their mission, as stated on their website, is to educate and advocate "around environmentally and socially responsible choices for individuals, schools, and communities. We seek to promote global sustainability by identifying and eliminating toxic exposures that permeate our lives and threaten public and environmental health."[10]

Included in the TTG initiatives is Project Green Prom sponsored by Whole Foods Market, which sells natural and organic products. The endeavor encourages U.S. high school students to use hair products, makeup, nail polish, and skin and body care products that are made in a sustainable way. The Green Prom effort also provides ideas for green prom dresses and tuxedoes, transportation, flowers, and foods. For example, some teenagers buy their attire at thrift stores or at Whole Foods, where donated outfits are for sale.

Another TTG initiative is Project Green Dorm, which involves high school and college students and encourages them to buy or use such items as organic bedding, preowned furniture, low-flow showerheads, green school supplies and clothing, and recycled materials in their rooms at home or in dorm rooms. There is a toolkit to initiate Project Green Dorm at the TTG website (www. teensturninggreen.org/events/project-green-dorm.html).

> ## School Supplies
>
> Students looking for green school supplies can find them in numerous stores today. For example, students can buy pens made with recycled materials, recycled ink cartridges for printers, paper made from post-consumer-recycled content, and other items. Such items as solar backpacks that recharge electronics and backpacks made from hemp or recycled materials are available as well.

percent. In addition, the Green Schools Program encourages and equips students to promote the lessons of energy efficiency in their homes and communities."[9]

Constructing Green School Buildings

In Greensburg, Kansas (yes, that's the name of the town), everyone is aware of what it means to construct green buildings, from schools to hospitals. Unfortunately, it all began with a tornado in 2007 that devastated nearly 96 percent of the farm community of about 1,400 residents. But the town rebuilt as a green and sustainable community with the help of teenagers like Taylor Schmidt. In a 2008 interview with Kenny Luna of *Treehugger*, Schmidt reports,

Kids have been the driving force for rebuilding. It's practically unprecedented. . . . Almost all of the youth have become involved in the rebuilding of Greensburg. We've been on committees with FEMA (Federal Emergency Management Agency) and there are around 20 students out of 100 involved on various committees and things like that. And because of that involvement a green club has formed at Greensburg High School. Basically it's a group of kids that want to learn more about green, what it is, how simple it is, how we can implement it in our lives. And what affect it has on our lives, finances, and the city. . . . I don't think you can find a person in the whole high school who doesn't know about going green.

When asked in the interview how Greensburg teenagers have helped the older generation in the town learn about the green concept, Schmidt explains that highschoolers have

gone with several of our teachers up to Chicago to the national green building convention and learned about how we can rebuild school and town with green roofs for water, and other practices ranging from all sorts of simple things like using efficient lighting and efficient water usage to installing wind turbines and solar and geothermal heating. . . . It's going to be a sustainable, lasting, innovative, comfortable, and inspiring atmosphere that encourages education and works with the environment instead of against it. That's what the entire town is trying to do; work with nature instead of against it. I think of myself as a 17-year old watching our town learn about how we can thrive again and even grow back better than we were before. Some people think how terrible it must be, but I think it's a blessing to live in such exciting times.[11]

As a result of the rebuilding, "Greensburg has more eco-friendly buildings than anywhere in the country, according to guidelines set by the Leadership in Energy and Environmental Design (LEED)." For example, "The Kiowa County School uses geothermal and wind energy, and it was built with reclaimed lumber from Hurricane Katrina and Kansas barns." The hospital also "runs on 100 percent renewable energy 100 percent of the time."[12]

The U.S. Green Building Council (USGBC) established the LEED certification program, which measures design, construction, and operation of green buildings. Along with the Greensburg example, many other schools across the nation are being certified.

In Virginia, Henrico County's two newest schools—Glen Allen High School and Holman Middle School—recently earned LEED certification, according to the local newspaper. Glen Allen High School "features an abundance of natural light, and . . . is modeled to require 28 percent less energy" than a design meeting the minimal building code; "a 50,000-gallon cistern collects storm water from the roof, which is reused for flushing.

It's a Fact

Global Green USA is the American affiliate of Green Cross International. The latter was launched in 1993 by former U.S.S.R. president Mikhail S. Gorbachev to foster a global effort toward a sustainable and secure future by reconnecting humanity with the environment.

This cistern, combined with low-plumbing fixtures, results in an 80 percent water use reduction versus a school using standard plumbing systems."[13]

Global Green USA, which works to create sustainable urban environments and combat global warming through green housing and schools, points out in its 2009 report that "green schools are smart economic investments for our communities, our children, and our planet. . . . The potential small increase in construction costs for a green school is paid back multiple times over the life of the building. Furthermore, as more high performance schools are built, design and construction costs will decrease while energy and water savings will increase." One of the most important benefits of a green school is student academic achievement. One study covered "more than 2000 classrooms in three school districts" and found that "students with the most classroom daylight progressed 20% faster in one year on math tests and 26% faster on reading tests than those students who learned in environments that received the least amount of natural light."[14]

High School Training for Green Jobs

With green projects implemented in many U.S. schools, some students are apt to want information about and training for green jobs and careers, which are expected to increase in the years ahead. The jobs could be in traditional trades like construction but might require training in installing solar panels, as an example. Some students may opt for careers in fields ranging from agriculture to zoology—with a focus on protecting the environment and sustainable practices. To determine which path to take toward a green job, high school students may get involved with programs that combine education and jobs skills training, such as these:

- In California, Career Partnership Academies within high schools integrate academic and career education and offer internships in green occupations. Partners in these endeavors include industries, businesses, and government agencies like the Environmental Protection Agency (EPA).

- In New Mexico, the Green Chamber provides students with real-world, hands-on experience and exposure to green jobs. New Mexico Green Chamber businesses offer on-site classes in the areas of PV installation, residential energy efficiency, and forest restoration.

- In Detroit, Michigan, eighty students working through the Conservation Leadership Corps (CLC) take part in a six-week program to maintain local parks by developing new trails and removing invasive species. While the students learn job skills, they also receive training in resume writing, interviewing, and personal finance. Johnson Controls, one of the sponsors of the CLC, holds a professional development day in which students "learn more about Johnson Controls' business units as well as how sustainability, energy efficiency, and renewable resources are an important part of doing business."[15]

- In Massachusetts, six high school students from Somerset, New Bedford, and Fall River were chosen to take part in a 2009 Youth Corps program that offers summer jobs through green projects at a nature center. The teenagers "painted buildings, cleared walking trails, harvested organic vegetables, tested the quality of water flowing into the Fall River drinking water supply, rebuilt stone walls, and planted trees." One of the teenagers,

Chelsea Sander, explains that she had been "exposed to so many different tools I had never had experience with before, starting with a lawn mower. That's always something my dad did." Another participant, Brittany Gentilucci, took younger students on nature walks and notes, "I learned a lot of different things about plants and animals, a lot about vernal pools and how to build bog bridges, and not only about many types of tools but how to use them. . . . I found it neat to be working with little kids and teaching them about things in their own backyard. They kept telling me that they loved it out here and were going to come back."[16] Many students who have taken part in the program have gone on to study for careers in environmental science, natural resource management, and other green professions.

- In the metropolitan area of Washington, D.C., a Green Jobs Corps has created a partnership between job training programs and green employers. Participants in the Greater Washington Green Jobs Corps are poor youth who face barriers to jobs and also blue-collar workers who are retrained for green jobs. The program focuses first on life skills sessions and then provides technical training, such as weatherizing homes, installing solar panels, and conducting energy audits.

- In Pittsburgh, Pennsylvania, students ages eighteen to twenty-four join the Mon Valley Environmental Innovative Training Program, which trains young people to work in hazardous waste operations. The program is designed to help students get "green jobs" or earn a college degree in an environmental discipline. Before going to college, Alesia Miller was undecided about what type of green career to pursue but notes the program was "something I believe will put me ahead in the work force."[17]

- In New York City, high school students from Brooklyn, Queens, and Manhattan received paid internships during the summer of 2011 to work on conservation through Leaders in Environmental Action for the Future (LEAF). But the students did not stay on the east coast. Rather, they

Choosing a Green College

Founded in 2005, the nonprofit Sustainable Endowments Institute (SEI) is "engaged in research and education to advance sustainability in campus operations and endowment practices."[18] Each year the institute issues a College Sustainability Report Card, which provides sustainability (or green) profiles for hundreds of colleges in all states and Canada. Each school evaluated receives an overall grade that is a grade point average for nine different categories: administration, climate change and energy, food and recycling, green building (meeting LEED standards), transportation, student involvement, endowment transparency, investment priorities, and shareholder engagement. The categories are explained and grades for schools are posted on SEI's interactive website at www. greenreportcard.org. For example, Luther College in Decorah, Iowa, received an A in the climate change and energy category because it has "reduced greenhouse gas emissions 20 percent since 2003 and is committed to a 50 percent reduction by 2012. The college has employed energy conservation measures such as temperature setbacks, energy management systems, electric metering, energy-efficient lighting, and vending machine sensors. Luther also generates geothermal energy on campus."[19] The overall grade for Luther was an A.

On the SEI website, a college or university can be compared to any other school among the more than three hundred listed. The 2011 overall grade for Brown University was an A compared to Harvard University, which received an A-; Bryn Mawr College received a B+; and the University of Oklahoma received a C. Those grades can change from one year to the next.

were sent to the Midwest to work alongside Waukesha County, Wisconsin, student interns in the wilderness of southeast Wisconsin. There the group pulled weeds, marked trails, built fences, and thinned out saplings in nature conservancy preserves. The New York interns also had the opportunity to visit Wisconsin colleges and the nature conservancy office in Madison, where they learned about potential environmental jobs. The conservancy found that, after following the interns over the years, about 35 percent "went into jobs related to ecology."[20]

Toward a Green Career

One way to explore a possible environmental or conservation career is to attend a Green Career Day. Such an event may be held on a college or university campus or in a city government building and is similar to a job fair. However, it may focus more on educating students and workers about the diverse aspects of green careers. Green Career Days demonstrate that environmental careers involve much more than working in national parks or recycling facilities. At a Green Career Days event, there could be a table or booth with an expert who describes clean technology or environmental law or journalism or nonprofit organizations working toward sustainability or other areas of sustainable development. Some representatives from green companies may discuss internships or job opportunities.

Just what kinds of green jobs might individuals represent? That can be a tricky question because there is no standard definition for what a green job is. And it is unlikely that any job is totally green. Suppose, for instance, a truck driver works for a company that manufactures turbines for wind power, and the driver delivers the turbines in a truck that runs on fossil fuel. The driver's job may be considered green, but perhaps the job would be greener if the truck was powered by an alternative fuel.

Some green jobs represented at Green Career events may be directly connected with the environment, such as conservation biologists, oceanographers, air quality specialists, and waste recyclers. Others may work behind the scenes, so to speak, such as accountants for green businesses, designers for eco-fashions, a scientist experimenting with biological controls for crop pests, or government officials who enforce green laws.

Alaska Youth for Environmental Action (AYEA), whose members have taken part in numerous presentations about global warming, sponsors a whole week

Off the Bookshelf

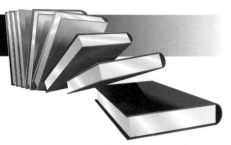

Dozens of books about green jobs and careers have been published since 2007. Some are introductory texts about green jobs; other books focus on specialties like jobs in green energy or sustainable agriculture. Titles include *Green Jobs: A Guide to Eco-Friendly Employment* (2008) by A. Bonwyn Llewellyn, James P. Hendrix, and K. C. Golden; *Green Careers: Choosing Work for a Sustainable Future* (2009) by Jim Cassio and Alice Rush; *The Complete Idiot's Guide to Green Careers* (2009) by Barbara Parks and Jodi Helmer; *Green Careers for Dummies* (2010) by Carol L. McLelland; *Green Collar Jobs: Environmental Careers for the 21st Century* by Scott M. Deitch; *Green Careers: You Can Make Money AND Save the Planet* (2010) by Jennifer Power Scott; *Jobs in Sustainable Agriculture* (2010) by Paula Johanson; *Legally Green: Careers in Environmental Law* (2011) by Susan Brophy; and many more. Such books are at bookstores, in libraries, and available online at such sites as Amazon, Barnes & Noble, Books-a-Million, Powell's, and BetterWorld Books.

---

about green careers, explaining what green jobs are and how teenagers can get them in the future. Part of the career week includes workshops on drafting a resume and learning how to be interviewed. During career week, experts, such as certified LEED architects and recyclers, are available to explain what they do. In addition teens who participate can spend a day with an individual who has a green job.

Along with its Green Schools Program, ASE also sponsors a program called Green Campus, which helps prepare college students for green jobs. The program trains about seventy-five interns each year. Renee Lafrenz, writing for ASE, states,

> More than four-fifths of the college student interns who participate in the Alliance's Green Campus Program go on to get jobs that support

sustainability. In fact, 83 percent of Green Campus graduates currently hold a "green job," defined as work that contributes substantially to preserving or restoring environmental quality. . . . The results are based on a survey of nearly seventy Green Campus alumni who graduated from 2005 through 2010.[21]

Heather Poiry, who participated in the ASE's Green Schools Program in high school and in the first Green Campus Program at the University of California, Merced, is "currently running her own solar energy company and nearing completion of a masters in engineering. Poiry feels like the program mentored her through her academic career, noting that 'I am now ready to give back to the world!'"[22]

Notes

1. Quoted in Jay Pateakos, "Green Jobs Place Teens in a Learning Environment," *Wicked Local Fall River/Herald News*, August 21, 2009, www.wickedlocal.com/fall-river/news/x772311147/Green-jobs-place-teens-in-a-learning-environment#axzz1d7hvoFQh (accessed November 8, 2011).

2. "Secondary School Green Team Projects," *King County*, June 3, 2011, http://your.kingcounty.gov/solidwaste/secondaryschool/gtprojects.asp (accessed July 31, 2011).

3. "2011 Earth Heroes at School," *King County*, April 14, 2011, http://your.kingcounty.gov/solidwaste/education/documents/EarthHero-winners-2011.pdf (accessed July 29, 2011).

4. "Green Your School Challenge," *DoSomething.org*, n.d., www.dosomething.org/green-your-school/sign-up/university-central-florida (accessed July 29, 2011).

5. Tom K., "City Academy Salt Lake City, Utah," *DoSomething.org*, April 21, 2011, www.dosomething.org/green-your-school/browse-schools?name=City%20Academy&zip=84102 (accessed July 30, 2011).

6. Emily B., "Milburn Senior High School," *DoSomething.org*, March 7, 2011, www.dosomething.org/green-your-school/browse-schools?name=Millburn%20Senior%20High%20School&zip=07041 (accessed July 30, 2011).

7. "Green Teens 2010–2011 Highlights," *Keep Austin Beautiful*, 2011, www.keepaustinbeautiful.org/GT2010-2011 (accessed August 3, 2011).

8. Ian Lally, Katie Blackmon, Leah Darlington, Tyler Meeks, "Olathe South Carpool Plan," *Kansas Green Schools*, September 2009, www.kansasgreenschools.org/files/Olathe%20South%20Carpool%20Plan%20Sept%202009.pdf (accessed August 4, 2011).

9. "Green Schools Program," *Alliance to Save Energy*, 2011, http://ase.org/programs/green-schools-program (accessed August 4, 2011).

10. "About," *Teens Turning Green*, 2011, www.teensturninggreen.org/about-us/about-us.html (accessed July 21, 2011).

11. Kenny Luna, "The TH Interview: Taylor Schmidt, Student at Greensburg High School," *Treehugger*, April 29, 2008, www.treehugger.com/files/2008/04/taylor-schmitt-th-interview-greenburg-kansas.php (accessed April 14, 2011).

12. Brian Mockenhaupt, "The Greening of Greensburg," *Readers Digest*, May 2011, p. 176.

13. "Holman and Glen Allen Earn LEED Certification," *Henrico Citizen*, July 12, 2011, www.henricocitizen.com/index.php/news/article/02190 (accessed July 30, 2011).

14. Global Green USA, *Healthier, Wealthier and Wiser: Global Green USA's Green Schools Report* (Santa Monica, CA: Global Green USA Headquarters, 2009), www.recycleworks.org/pdf/Greenschoolsreport-final.pdf (accessed August 1, 2011).

15. Melissa Hinchba-Ownby, "Detroit: Green Jobs for Teens," *Mother Nature Network*, July 12, 2010, www.mnn.com/money/green-workplace/blogs/detroit-green-jobs-for-teens (accessed July 31, 2011).

16. Jay Pateakos, "Green Jobs Place Teens in Learning Environment," *The Herald News*, August 20, 2009, www.heraldnews.com/news/local_news/x769901970/Green-jobs-place-teens-in-a-learning-environment (accessed August 1, 2011).

17. Jodi Weigand, "Training Program Gives Students Boost toward 'Green' Careers," *Pittsburgh Tribune Review*, July 11, 2011, www.pittsburghlive.com/x/pittsburghtrib/news/s_746165.html# (accessed August 1, 2011).

18. Sustainable Endowments Institute, "Greening the Bottom Line on Campus," news release, February 9, 2011, www.endowmentinstitute.org/index.html (accessed November 8, 2011).

19. The College Sustainability Report Card, "Luther College," *Report Card 2011*, www.greenreportcard.org/report-card-2011/schools/luther-college (accessed November 8, 2011).

20. Rick Wood, "N.Y. Teens See a Different Side of Nature," *Milwaukee Journal Sentinel*, August 5, 2011, www.jsonline.com/news/waukesha/126931233.html (accessed August 7, 2011).

21. Renee Lafrenz, "Alliance Green Campus Program: Pathway to Green Careers," *Alliance to Save Energy*, April 28, 2011, http://ase.org/efficiencynews/alliance-green-campus-program-pathway-green-careers (August 4, 2011).

22. Renee Lafrenz, "Alliance Green Campus Program: Pathway to Green Careers," *Alliance to Save Energy*, April 28, 2011, http://ase.org/efficiencynews/alliance-green-campus-program-pathway-green-careers (accessed August 4, 2011).

BEING GREEN
AT HOME

···

*"I try to be as environmentally friendly as I can. It just means I keep the doors closed
to drafty rooms, shut off lights and computers when done with them, and keep the room
temperature at a reasonable level, and offset it with my family's wood stove."*
—Nick Shigao, a Connecticut high school junior[1]

Repeatedly, the advice for living green includes using eco-friendly products, reducing food and other waste, reusing manufactured goods whenever possible, recycling, conserving energy, and reducing water usage. All of those actions apply at home. For example, installing a low-flow showerhead reduces water consumption. So does hand washing dishes, if you refrain from letting the water run while rinsing each piece.

Certainly not everyone can afford energy-saving measures, such as solar panels for their home or new windows and doors that insulate against heat and cold or gray-water recycling systems. But little things help. High school senior Amisha Sisodiya opines, "I don't think I'm overall eco-friendly, but I try to recycle and turn off the lights to conserve energy."[2]

Teenager Jonathan Regaldo of San Antonio, Texas, takes a variety of actions to be green at home. One is recycling organic material, such as garbage, dead leaves, and grass, to create a compost that breaks down and returns nutrients to the soil.

In the spring of 2011, the teen staff of *LA Youth*, a newspaper by and about teens, took on a challenge to reduce air pollution by using less energy for one week. Obviously, leaving the car at home and walking or bicycling would be helpful

For some people, being green at home means conserving water, as this young woman demonstrates by brushing her teeth with the water turned off when it's not needed.

because emissions from vehicles contribute to smog in the Los Angeles area. The teens also were advised to take action at home: unplug electronics, turn off lights, and take short showers because the power plants that generate electricity for heating, cooling, and running machinery and appliances emit air pollutants. The teenagers all thought they could handle the challenge, but at times it wasn't easy. For example, to save energy, Quinten tried walking to school but was late for first period and "got detention." The next day he was able to carpool with his mom when she went to work. But some other activities, like taking short showers and turning off lights when leaving a room, were more difficult than he expected. He notes, "By Thursday, I was finally getting the hang of turning off the lights when I left a room. . . . Although I didn't meet my expectations, I changed habits and I feel good about it. If I reduce the energy I use, there will be less pollution and everyone benefits from that."[3]

Shefali reports, "Many times, I have tried to go green by recycling or reusing bags, but these things never lasted long enough to become a routine." She adds that she "turned off the lights when I wasn't using them and unplugged the TV, chargers and computer every night. My hope is that the things I did this one-week challenge will become routine."[4]

For Tracy, "the simplest part was turning off the lights when I left the room and unplugging electronics when they weren't in use. Another easy part for me was using the clothesline because my family already uses it to save energy. When I did my laundry, the sunlight was so bright that my clothes dried a lot faster than using the dryer." But she reports, "The hardest thing was making sure that my computer was turned off. Sometimes I keep the computer on for a long time even if I'm not using it and that wastes power. So I tried to do the computer part of my homework at one time and then switch it off. Then I would do the rest of my homework that didn't need a computer, like math or science."[5]

For Aaron the challenge helped him develop the "habit of turning off lights and unplugging appliances after I used them. Any time I finished using a toaster, lamp, phone charger, computer, or a light I immediately unplugged it."[6]

Jessica reports that taking a short shower was difficult, but during the challenge she managed to take fifteen-minute showers rather than her "usual 30-minute showers. . . . I used to stand there and let the water run on me, relaxing and thinking back on the day. My main goal was to get in and out of the shower as quickly as possible."[7]

Kiera thought she had a plan to save energy. She awoke early to open all the blinds in her home and hoped that would convince family members to use the daylight rather than turn on electric lights. She writes, "I thought it was a fool-proof plan, but I was wrong." She was frustrated that her family did not make an effort to help out and conserve energy. . . . I tried my hardest to remind them about turning off their lights, but nothing seemed to work. This challenge opened my eyes to how much energy my family uses for no reason. I learned how important it is to do my part in helping conserve energy and help others as well in conserving energy because they won't do it themselves, and it still needs to be done.[8]

Conserving Energy

Conserving energy is an important part of being green at home, and that has prompted many families to buy energy-efficient appliances from microwaves to refrigerators. If you have a refrigerator without the Energy Star label, you can still save energy by

- keeping the fridge away from heat vents or windows that allow direct sunlight,
- closing the door quickly rather than leaving it open for long periods,
- collecting all items that need refrigeration on a counter before opening the refrigerator door,
- checking the gasket seal to make sure the door closes tightly,
- setting the refrigerator temperature at 36°F to 38°F, and
- setting the freezer at the factory-recommended temperature.

To summarize the suggestions to reduce energy consumption that the *LA Youth* has reported, turn off the lights when you leave a room, turn off or unplug electric appliances, use less water, reuse or recycle plastic bags, and when possible ride a bike or walk rather than drive a vehicle to get to and from your home.

In addition, try these energy savers:

- Use rechargeable batteries.

- Microwave food when possible rather than heat or cook on a stove or in an oven.
- Reduce heat and cool-air leaks around windows and doors with caulking or weather stripping.
- Stop plumbing leaks.
- When laundering clothes use full loads or set the washing machine for the appropriate size of the load.
- Use the proper dryer setting or dry clothes on a rack or clothesline outdoors or in the basement, laundry room, or garage. (Those clothes softener sheets can be reused to clean streaks from mirrors.)
- Change your air filters once a month or every third month if you have a three-month filter.
- Use timers for outside and indoor lights.
- Open the drapes or blinds to let the sun in during cold months and block the sun during hot days.

Less Paper at Home

Advocates for living green no doubt are recycling newspapers and other types of paper products and reducing paper usage at home. But junk mail can be difficult to control. Nearly five million tons of it are sent out each year. A CBS correspondent reports that "Americans receive nearly 90 billion pieces of advertising mail every year." Some of it can be recycled in places where mixed paper products are collected. Or junk mail can be reduced. One method for first-class mail is to mark an *unopened* envelope by crossing off your address and writing "return to sender" with an arrow pointing to the sender's address. Another is to stuff an addressed, *stamped* envelope with the senders' advertisements or political messages and mail it back.

If you fill out questionnaires and so-called contest forms that include your mailing address, chances are you will get catalogs or flyers in the mail advertising various merchandise. So if you don't want that type of mail, don't fill out the

U.S. Water Usage at Home

According to the U.S. Geological Survey, *each* American uses about eighty to one hundred gallons of water per day. If you have ever seen gallons of drinking water lining store shelves, you have some idea how much water a person uses daily. Of course, you would not drink that much water. But when you take into account household use, the largest use is flushing the toilet. Charles Fishman, author of *The Big Thirst*, writes, "The typical American flushes the toilet five times a day at home, and uses 18.5 gallons of water just for that. What that means is that every day, Americans flush 5.7 billion gallons of clean drinking water down the toilet. And that's just at home."[9]

questionnaires. Two websites also can help: *Catalog Choice* (catalogchoice.org) and *DMAchoice* (DMAchoice.org).

To help reduce paper in your home, use a computer (if possible) to e-mail rather than use paper to send such messages as invitations, announcements, or thank-you notes. Use both sides of printer paper or do not print out computer-generated materials unless absolutely necessary. Reuse paper bags as wrappings for packages that must be sent by mail. Use shredded paper for protective packing materials. Reuse file folders whenever possible. Cut scrap paper into note-sized pieces to reuse for lists or messages; the backs of used envelopes can serve the same purpose. Decorate gift packages with a newspaper's colorful comic-strip pages. Instead of disposable paper containers, substitute reusable mugs, plates, bowls, and utensils; use cloth napkins or paper towels with a high postconsumer recycled content.

Cleaning Naturally

Many cleaning products claim to be "natural," "chemical free," and "nonirritating." But according to *Consumer Reports*, the claims have little meaning because they are vague or cannot be verified. (You can search labels by the logo or label category, by product category, or by certifier on *Consumer Reports'* website at www .greenerchoices.org/eco-labels.)

For natural, nontoxic household cleaners that could be in your home already, you might opt for lemons, white vinegar, baking soda, and borax (sodium borate). Lemon juice will clean copper and brass. Mix white vinegar and lemon juice for a stain remover. A paste of baking soda and water cleans and deodorizes surfaces in the kitchen and bathroom. Undiluted white vinegar is a natural toilet bowl cleaner. One-half cup each of white vinegar and baking soda followed by boiling water acts as a foaming drain cleaner. Borax will clean, deodorize, and disinfect— it softens water and cleans wallpaper, painted walls, and floors.

Many personal care and household cleaners claim to be natural or made from organic ingredients, but the claims could be greenwashing if the products include synthetic materials, which can be toxic. So what do you look for when checking out products?

For cosmetics, personal care, and household cleaners, there are nontoxic products that carry a "leaping bunny" logo—a rabbit leaping upward. The logo means that companies using it are cruelty free—they have not tested their finished product or formulas on animals, and they do not use animal products in their ingredients. A list of those companies appears on the website for the Coalition for Consumer Information on Cosmetics (www.leapingbunny.org/images/cciclist .pdf). Many of the listed companies also claim that their products are organic or natural and contain no sulfates such as sodium lauryl sulfate (a detergent); parabens (preservatives); phthalates (chemicals that fix fragrances in a product); or petroleum-based ingredients. To check out what companies say about the ingredients they use, try searching the Internet by company name or do some investigating in stores by reading labels on personal care products or household cleaners.

Cleaning the indoor air at your home can be a green matter—literally. Green plants are natural air filters, and *Mother Nature Network* suggests more than one dozen plants to improve air quality. Photos of them appear on their website (www .mnn.com/health/healthy-spaces/photos/15-houseplants-for-improving-indoor-air-quality). Some examples include the following:

- The snake plant (*Sansevieria trifasciata*), also called mother-in-law's tongue, filters out formaldehyde, a gas that is used in many household products, particle board, glues, permanent press fabrics, and personal care products. The plant can survive in low light and moist conditions, such as in a bathroom.
- Golden pathos, or devil's ivy (*Scindapsus aures*), is a vine that also filters formaldehyde and stays green when kept in the dark.
- Aloe (*Aloe vera*) is a succulent that cleans the air of numerous chemicals, and aloe gel helps heal burns and cuts; the gel is an ingredient used in numerous personal care products.
- Peace lily (*Spathiphyllum*) removes volatile organic compounds (VOCs), gaseous chemicals found in paints and lacquers, paint strippers, cleaning supplies, pesticides, building materials and furnishings, such office equipment as copiers and printers, correction fluids and carbonless copy paper, graphics and craft materials like glues and adhesives, permanent markers, and photographic solutions, according to the Environmental Protection Agency (EPA). VOCs can cause eye, nose, and throat irritation; headaches; loss of coordination; nausea; and liver, kidney, and central nervous system damage.
- Heart leaf philodendron (*Philodendron oxycardium*) also removes VOCs, but it is poisonous when eaten by pets or small children.

Being Green Outside the Home

Across the United States, families living green are creating urban gardens. One of the most publicized is the garden planted on the south lawn of the White

House. Beginning in 2009, First Lady Michelle Obama began overseeing school children as they planted and harvested vegetables, berries, and herbs in her effort to promote locally grown food and more healthful eating.

The Obama White House is not the first to engage in gardening on site. During the early 1800s, U.S. presidents grew their own food. Thomas Jefferson, who served from 1801 to 1809, was an avid gardener. He wanted to plant vegetables near the president's house (the modern-day White House), but the land was swampy and not suitable for gardening. Later, as the land was filled in, gardeners planted fruit trees, vegetable gardens, and herb gardens near the White House. Workers built a greenhouse there in 1857. The greenhouse stood until 1902.

In 1943, during World War II (1939–1945), the federal government reserved large amounts of food for soldiers and rationed, or limited, sales of food to civilians. First Lady Eleanor Roosevelt encouraged Americans to grow "victory gardens" or "relief gardens" in their backyards to provide their own fresh produce. More than twenty million Americans complied.

Even today urban gardens often are called "victory gardens," but they are more likely to be symbols of living green. The urban gardening movement is growing—no pun intended. Increasingly, people in urban areas are digging up their lawns or vacant land in cities to plant vegetables and fruits. In Florida, one man in Clearwater plowed his entire one-acre yard to plant a garden and four citrus trees, build a greenhouse and yard houses for ducks and chickens, and create a fish pond for tilapia.

One gardener in West Columbia, South Carolina, Sarah Rosenbaum, "ripped up about a quarter of her family's landscaped yard to install six raised vegetable beds. . . . The project got under way in early March when Ms. Rosenbaum, her partner and his twelve-year-old twins started seeds indoors for all their vegetables—from bok choy to zucchini."[10]

For many urban residents, there is not much space for gardening, but in some neighborhoods with single-family homes, owners are replacing their front lawns with edible gardens—planting vegetables, fruits, and herbs. For people who

What Do You Think?

Is a green lawn actually a sign of living green? Having a green lawn is the ideal for many U.S. home owners, especially suburbanites. Green-lawn lovers want to be the envy of their neighbors, and they likely spend a great deal of time and money to create a manicured, weed-free, carpetlike or turflike lawn. Author Ted Steinberg asks "Why are Americans so obsessed with their lawns?" in his book *American Green: The Obsessive Quest for the Perfect Lawn* (2006). The answer in part comes from history.

Until the late eighteenth century, green, weed-free lawns were rare in the United States. Most Americans lived in rural areas, and outside their homes was a front yard of packed dirt or perhaps a small garden with herbs and vegetables. When Americans began traveling to Europe, they observed lawns of wealthy homeowners and city parks and other areas with expanses of green grass. Americans wanted the same for their communities. After all, several U.S. presidents had green lawns on their estates, and the grass was "mowed" by sheep and other grazing livestock. The average American, however, could not afford a vast estate or the livestock to keep the lawn trimmed.

By the late 1800s and early 1900s, as grass seed, lawn mowers, and sprinkling systems were being mass produced, green lawns became popular and affordable. But getting the right kind of seed for the varied U.S. climates was no simple matter, so in 1915, the U.S. Department of Agriculture (USDA) worked with the Golf Association to investigate the types of grasses that would create attractive lawns nationwide. Fifteen years later a mixture of grasses proved to be acceptable to the American climate. Then the American Garden Club, through widespread publicity, persuaded home owners that having a beautiful green lawn was a civic duty. The Garden Club even set strict guidelines for the height of the grass, demanding a single type of grass with no weeds and edges of lawns trimmed neatly.

After World War II (1948–1952), Abraham Levitt and his sons built Levittown on Long Island, New York. Each house in this first American suburb had a green lawn already growing and thriving when owners moved in. With the return of veterans, suburban communities grew, and green lawns became increasingly important as status symbols. Sales of chemical fertilizers and herbicides proliferated. Continued use of fertilizers and pesticides made lawns appear perfect, but the chemicals and toxins in such lawns have leached into water supplies and also threatened the health of people and pets, as well as bees and birds.

Currently, nontoxic fertilizers and herbicides are available, and environmental groups strongly encourage their use. Yet, producing a green lawn is not for everyone who wants to live green, as home owners who landscape with native plants or vegetable gardens have shown. In addition, some home owners spray paint their lawns green when grass is dormant or during droughts. And it is not unusual to see a home with a front yard of cement painted green or an installation of synthetic turf in the yard and outdoor areas. Companies that claim to make eco-friendly artificial grass say it is produced from recycled plastics and requires no watering, thus saving energy, and it is 100 percent recyclable after long use. But manufacturing the product does involve extensive energy use.

So what do you think? Is green grass, whether fake or real, a symbol of living green?

live in apartment buildings, the solution often is to grow foods like peppers or tomatoes in pots, buckets, or other containers placed on apartment balconies or on fire escape landings or to create rooftop gardens. Food also can be grown in such throwaway items as used tires, kiddie pools, and leaky watering cans. Gardeners may tier their plants, growing those that need shade below plants that need sun. Raised garden beds are another possibility for urbanites—these can be built and placed on patios. Because plants grow closer together in the raised beds, they may produce up to twice the amount of vegetables as a regular garden plot.

For homes with yards that require mowing, the green way would be to grasscycle. That means leaving the grass clippings on the lawn. Some home owners think that is unsightly, but grass clippings contain nitrogen and reduce the amount of fertilizer needed. In fact, chemical fertilizers often are overused and can run off

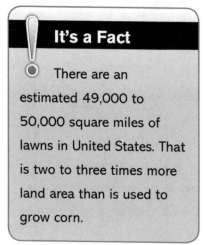

It's a Fact

There are an estimated 49,000 to 50,000 square miles of lawns in United States. That is two to three times more land area than is used to grow corn.

lawns and into streams, polluting the water and threatening aquatic life. According to the U.S. National Wildlife Federation, more than seventy tons of fertilizers and pesticides are added to American lawns and gardens every year.

Instead of green lawns, some home owners landscape with native plants that require less maintenance (no mowing, for example) than grass; usually resist drought; and reduce the need for fertilizers, pesticides, and water. However, in some communities, home-owner associations forbid such landscaping and demand that lawns be kept green even during times of severe drought—or face a fine.

Reducing Food Waste

It is time to clean out the refrigerator. Out goes some cauliflower that is beginning to grow sprouts. That leftover carryout meal has been there for more than a week, so it, too, becomes a throwaway. The half-empty carton of milk smells funky—out it goes. The yogurt has exceeded its "best-used-by" date. It, too, is tossed. Then there are foods such as the stale donuts on the kitchen counter. Some apples in a fruit basket are bruised—one is mushy and brown. An orange is dried up and shriveled. All these items become garbage.

Examples such as these are common in kitchens across the United States. Individuals and households often don't realize just how much food they throw away every day, notes the EPA. According to a 2006 study, American households throw away 14 percent of the food they purchase, an average of 470 pounds of food, annually. This costs a family of four nearly $600 per year.

By taking some simple steps, individuals and households can significantly reduce the amount of food and money wasted every year, and the EPA advises

Much food waste comes from fast food leftovers that become garbage along with their containers.

people to visit their household food waste page (www.epa.gov/osw/conserve/materials/organics/food/fd-house.htm). The following are some small efforts that can make a big difference in reducing food waste:

- Make lists and stick to them when grocery shopping.
- Use leftovers as ingredients for new meals. Turn leftover cooked chicken into chicken salad, for instance.
- Serve smaller portions.
- Compost food scraps. (See www.epa.gov/osw/conserve/rrr/greenscapes/pubs/compost-guide.pdf for a guide.)
- Put dates on carryout containers to remind yourself to eat the food quickly before it spoils.
- Buy small packages of fresh foods rather than large packages that might spoil before they're completely eaten.

Dumpster Divers

The practice doesn't appeal to most people, but dumpster divers have no qualms about what they do: They dive into dumpsters for food—not rotten food but packaged and edible foods. They call themselves freegans or urban foragers and live on food that others throw away, digging into supermarket, restaurant, or convenience store dumpsters to salvage food items. Actually, the dumpster divers may use long poles or other equipment to search for food and things that they can salvage and sell for recycling. Some live by an anticonsumerism philosophy and practice minimal consumption of consumer goods. Others simply want to save on food costs.

In Goshen, Indiana, a group of students at Goshen College have taken part in dumpster diving. They pay for some of their food, but they also have salvaged large amounts of tomatoes, which were turned into tomato sauce for pasta dishes; eggplants that provided the basis for many meals; and many unopened packages of bread. They also found "roasted chickens still steaming with heat. Fruit salvaged from whole bags scrapped because of one bad apple. Packaged meat, especially in the winter, when low temps keep it from spoiling. Milk and yogurt. Potato chips and crackers still in their packaging." One of the dumpster divers, Rody Matthews, explains, "As long as it doesn't smell bad or taste bad, I'll eat it. . . . Usually I'll just go by my nose." Another student explains that dumpster diving is a "good way to reduce food costs and also reduce our impact on the planet."[11]

Is dumpster diving illegal? That depends on the community. Laws vary, but in Goshen, Indiana, it is legal to remove items from a dumpster if it is along a street, alley, or area waiting for trash pickup. But if the container, such as a recycling bin, is located near a home on private property, it is illegal to forage items from it. On the other hand, laws in some areas of the country prohibit dumpster diving altogether.

- Make smoothies out of fruit that is getting overripe.

- Place newly purchased food items toward the back of a cupboard or refrigerator and pull older items forward so they will be used first.

- Freeze portions of meals for eating later.

- Donate leftover party food to a food bank or kitchen.

- Share a meal with an elderly neighbor or friend.

Notes

1. Quoted in Shemona Singh, Joseph A. Foran, and Esha Deshmuh, "Teens Work to Reduce Carbon Footprint," ctpost.com, March 29, 2011, http://www.ctpost.com/living/article/Teens-work-to-reduce-carbon-footprint-1309575.php (accessed November 8, 2011).

2. Quoted in Shemona Singh, Joseph A. Foran, and Esha Deshmuh, "Teens Work to Reduce Carbon Footprint," ctpost.com, March 29, 2011, http://www.ctpost.com/living/article/Teens-work-to-reduce-carbon-footprint-1309575.php (accessed November 8, 2011).

3. "Let's Cut Down on Air Pollution," *LA Youth*, March/April 2011, www.layouth.com/lets-cut-down-on-air-pollution (accessed July 6, 2011).

4. "Let's Cut Down on Air Pollution," *LA Youth*, March/April 2011, www.layouth.com/lets-cut-down-on-air-pollution (accessed July 6, 2011)

5. "Let's Cut Down on Air Pollution," *LA Youth*, March/April 2011, www.layouth.com/lets-cut-down-on-air-pollution (accessed July 6, 2011).

6. "Small Steps to Clean Air," *LA Youth*, March/April 2011, www.layouth.com/small-steps-to-clean-air-part-2 (accessed August 11, 2011).

7. "Small Steps to Clean Air," *LA Youth*, March/April 2011, www.layouth.com/small-steps-to-clean-air-part-3 (accessed July 6, 2011).

8. "Small Steps to Clean Air," *LA Youth*, March/April 2011, www.layouth.com/small-steps-to-clean-air-part-2 (accessed July 6, 2011).

9. Charles Fishman, "The Revenge of Water," from *The Big Thirst*, *The Week*, July 29, 2011, p. 40.

10. Anne Marie Chaker, "The Vegetable Patch Takes Root," *Wall Street Journal*, June 5, 2008, p. D1, http://online.wsj.com/article/SB121262319456246841.html (accessed August 25, 2009).

11. Tim Vandenack, "Dumpster Diving Isn't for Everyone," *Elkhart Truth*, August 3, 2008, www.etruth.com/Know/News/Story.aspx?ID=457760 (accessed August 10, 2011).

LIVING GREEN TODAY AND TOMORROW

··

"The generation most affected by climate change is standing up to let the world know that
our future matters more than profits and conveniences."
—*Alec Loorz, youth leader for the iMatter March*[1]

To quote another student, Mia Szarvas, president of her school's Sustainability Club, "We want action . . . now because we want a livable future."[2] Action is also what Alec Loorz of Oak View, California, expects. Loorz is the organizer of iMatter March, which began on May 7, 2011, and extended through the summer and early fall of 2011. Loorz explains, "iMatter is not an event. This is a movement. . . . Over 150 marches to compel our leaders to LEAD AS IF OUR FUTURE MATTERS are registered on the map in over 35 countries."[3] Besides the march, Loorz and other young people in fifty states filed lawsuits demanding the federal government act now to curb global warming. Loorz explains, "We don't have political power. We don't have the money to compete with corporate lobbyists. We can't vote. All we have is our voice."[4]

Teens Plan for the Future

With all the demands on today's teens, who has time to prepare for a green future? Ally Maize of the Green Youth Movement believes that, no matter how busy teens are, there still is time "to care about our future, especially when there are simple ways to make a difference. After all, today's teens are inheriting the earth, we

Off the Bookshelf

If you are looking for information about how to be an activist now or in the future, *The Young Activist's Guide to Building a Green Movement + Changing the World* by Sharon J. Smith could be helpful. As the title indicates, this is a how-to book that provides practical information on the steps to take to become a green activist. Chapters cover such aspects as developing an action plan, communicating your message, gathering support, soliciting funds, getting publicity, and finally changing the world.

---

need to create change now."[5] Canadian Greg Ross of the Sierra Youth Coalition, affiliated with the Sierra Club of Canada, agrees. In his words,

> Teens are realizing that they will be the ones having to deal with all the environmental problems left behind from the older generation, and they are not going to wait around and do nothing. Our government's stewardship has been very weak and young people cannot trust or believe that the government will solve all the problems. Canada used to be viewed as an environmental leader and now. . . . We are heading in the wrong direction and young people do not want this to happen.[6]

How are teens preparing for the future? Some are learning how to be tomorrow's environmental entrepreneurs, or they are planning for a career in a green profession or job, such as environmental law, green architecture, and forestry. Or they are learning more about living green. For example, in 2011, Catawba College in Salisbury, North Carolina, held a National Environmental Summit for High School Students, which attracted students from across the United States. The summit focused on "building students' knowledge and skills around environmental sustainability, collaboration and communication."[7]

Other students plan ahead by attending workshops or conferences on sustainable agriculture, LEED-certified building, alternative energy, Green Ways to Move the Mail (a Smithsonian workshop for teens), and similar topics. Still others are learning trades, such as how to install green roofs, wind turbines, and energy-efficient equipment.

Checking What You Know about Living Green

No, this isn't a reading comprehension exam or an IQ test. It is simply a way to enhance your awareness of ecological issues. Questions 1 through 8 are adapted from a quiz by the National Park Service,[8] and 9 through 20 are adapted from a quiz by the Smithsonian National Zoological Park.[9] The answers are at the end of the quiz.

A Green Quiz

1. Which of the following can be recycled?
   A. Milk cartons
   B. Plastic water bottles
   C. Glass containers
   D. Paper bags
   E. All of the above
2. Who can recycle?
   A. Only city residents
   B. Almost everyone
   C. Only farmers
   D. Only taxpayers
3. If you recycle one ton of paper, how many trees can you save?
   A. One
   B. Nine

    C. Seventeen

    D. Thirty-five

4. How many times can glass be recycled?

    A. None

    B. Once

    C. Twenty times

    D. Forever

5. How many plastic bottles do Americans go through every year?

    A. 1.8 million

    B. 2.5 million

    C. 5.3 million

    D. 7.1 million

6. How much junk mail do Americans receive in one day?

    A. Enough to heat 250,000 homes

    B. Enough to power a TV for one year

    C. Enough to fill 10 square miles in a landfill

    D. 1,000 trees worth

7. The average aluminum can is made up of how much recycled aluminum?

    A. 10 percent

    B. 30 percent

    C. 50 percent

    D. 70 percent

8. Annually, how much plastic film does America produce?

    A. Enough to wrap up Alaska

    B. Enough to stretch around the world twice

    C. Enough to cover Connecticut

    D. Enough to shrink wrap Texas

9. Global warming may lead to

    A. More extreme weather events

    B. Rising sea levels

C. The extinction of many animal and plant species

D. All of the above

10. One Energy Star compact fluorescent lightbulb can

    A. Last ten times longer that an incandescent bulb

    B. Use two-thirds less energy

    C. Help save money on your electric bill

    D. Do all of the above

11. The Sierra Club is dedicated to preserving

    A. Night clubs in Las Vegas

    B. Natural resources

    C. Golf courses

    D. A discount warehouse

12. Rachel Carson wrote a best-selling book titled

    A. *Silent Majority*

    B. *Silent Night*

    C. *Silent Spring*

    D. *Silent Signals*

13. What is the primary focus of the book *An Inconvenient Truth?*

    A. Plagiarism

    B. Habitual liars

    C. Global warming

    D. Consumerism

14. Which of the following is a renewable resource?

    A. Oil

    B. Iron ore

    C. Trees

    D. Coal

15. Which of the following household materials is considered hazardous waste?

    A. Plastic packaging

    B. Glass

    C. Batteries

    D. Spoiled food

16. What is the *primary* reason that animals become extinct?

    A. People kill wildlife

    B. Loss of habitat

    C. They die of old age

    D. Floods

17. The average distance your food travels from the farm to the grocery store is

    A. 20 miles

    B. 500 miles

    C. 1,500 miles

    D. 3,000 miles

18. You can be more energy efficient at home by

    A. Setting your thermostat a little higher in the summer and a little lower in the winter

    B. Sealing air leaks around windows and doors

    C. Drying laundry on a clothesline

    D. All of the above

19. How many trees does it take annually to send junk mail to Americans?

    A. 50,000

    B. 100,000

    C. 1 million

    D. 100 million

20. If no plastic or paper bags were produced, we would

    A. Reduce air and water pollution

    B. Spare millions of trees

    C. Decrease oil use by millions of barrels

    D. All of the above

21. You can reduce your carbon footprint

    A. By driving the car whenever you can

B. By eating at fast food restaurants

C. By watching environmental videos

D. By riding a bike whenever possible

22. You protect wildlife when you

A. Join a protest against inhumane slaughter of seals

B. Read books about endangered species

C. Watch the Discovery Channel on TV

D. Create a compost

23. The best way to determine which products are truly green is

A. By watching commercials on TV

B. By getting advice from neighbors

C. By browsing the Internet

D. By looking for legitimate green certification logos

24. Used batteries should be

A. Thrown in the garbage

B. Exchanged for new ones at a store

C. Taken to a hazardous waste site

D. Burned in an incinerator

(Answers: 1-E; 2-B; 3-C; 4-D; 5-B; 6-A; 7-C; 8-D; 9-D; 10-D; 11-B; 12-C; 13-C; 14-C; 15-C; 16-B; 17-C; 18-D; 19-D; 20-D; 21-D; 22-A; 23-D; 24-C)

Call yourself "emerald green" if your answers were correct twenty to twenty-four times.

Call yourself "mostly green" if your answers were correct twelve to nineteen times.

Call yourself "light green" if your answers were correct six to eleven times.

Call yourself "wannabe green" if your answers were correct zero to five times.

Back to the opening question: What does living green really mean? In summary it means trying to "reduce, reuse, recycle" and making this slogan a meaningful part of everyday life. Add another *r* for *respect*: respecting and conserving our natural resources so they will be available in the future. Green ideas are found within this book and in the other resources listed.

Sometimes living green means taking small steps at first, as the Tulsa, Oklahoma, teenagers learned when they began planting trees—a few at a time until more than two thousand were in the ground. They declare, "It helps save the planet."[10]

One person alone cannot save the world, but one person can be joined by the green actions of hundreds, thousands, and millions of other people around the globe. Together we can help save the earth—and ourselves.

Notes

1. Alec Loorz, "Letter from Alec Loorz," *Kids vs. Global Warming*, 2011, http://imattermarch .org (accessed August 17, 2011).
2. Brett Wilkison, "Sebastopol Teens Organize March to Highlight Climate Change," *The Press Democrat*, May 8, 2011, www.pressdemocrat.com/article/20110508/ARTICLES/110509522 (accessed May 10, 2011).
3. Alec Loorz, "Our Climate, Our Future, Our Revolution,"*iMatter Youth Council*, 2011, http:// imattermarch.org (accessed May 18, 2011).
4. Marya Jones Barlow, "Teen Activist Plans 'Million Kid March' to Fight Global Warming," *Ventura County Star*, May 4, 2011, http://m.vcstar.com/news/2011/may/04/teen-activist- plans-145million-kid-march-to (accessed May 18, 2011).
5. Holly Ashworth, "Why Should Teens Go Green?" *About.com*, 2011, http://teenadvice.about .com/od/stayinghappy/a/ways_that_teens_can_go_green.htm (accessed August 18, 2011).
6. Vanessa Campisi, "Teens Unite for the Planet," *GreenLiving*, 2011, www.greenlivingonline .com/article/teens-unite-planet (August 18, 2011).
7. Valaida Fullwood, "Summit Turns Teens Green: An Interview with John Wear," *Charlotte Viewpoint*, July 26, 2011, www.charlotteviewpoint.org/article/2478/Summit-turns-teens- green---An-interview-with--John (accessed August 18, 2011).
8. Jillian Richie, "Recycling Quiz," *National Park Service*, n.d., www.nps.gov/anch/upload/ RecyclingQuizFinal.pdf (accessed October 23, 2011).
9. "How Green Are You?" *Smithsonian National Zoological Park*, n.d., http://nationalzoo.si.edu/ Publications/GreenTeam/GreenQuiz.cfm (accessed October 23, 2011).
10. "Three Teenagers Work to Save the Planet," *2 Works for You*, December 16, 2010, www.kjrh .com/dpp/news/problem_solvers/three-teenagers-work-to-save-the-planet (accessed August 14, 2011).

Selected Resources

Books

Bach, David. *Go Green, Live Rich* (New York: Broadway Books/Random House, 2008).

Carson, Rachel. *Silent Spring* (New York: Mariner Books, 2002).

Cassio, Jim, and Alice Rush. *Green Careers: Choosing Work for a Sustainable Future* (Gabriola Island, BC: New Society, 2009).

Connor, Nancy. *Living Green: The Missing Manual* (Sebastopol, CA: O'Reilly Media, 2009).

Deitch, Scott M. *Green Collar Jobs: Environmental Careers for the 21st Century* (Santa Barbara, CA: ABC-CLIO, 2010).

Freinkel, Susan. *Plastic: A Toxic Love Story* (New York: Houghton Mifflin Harcourt, 2011).

Gore, Al. *An Inconvenient Truth: The Crisis of Global Warming* (New York: Penguin Group, 2007).

Hohn, Donovan. *Moby-Duck: The True Story of 28,800 Bath Toys Lost at Sea and of the Beachcombers, Oceanographers, Environmentalists, and Fools, Including the Author, Who Went in Search of Them* (New York: Viking, 2011).

Kaye, Cathryn Berger, and Philippe Cousteau. *Going Blue: A Teen Guide to Saving Our Oceans, Lakes, Rivers, and Wetlands* (Minneapolis, MN: Free Spirit, 2010).

Lewis, Barbara. *The Teen Guide to Global Action: How to Connect with Others (Near and Far) to Create Social Change* (Minneapolis, MN: Free Spirit, 2008).

Llewellyn, A. Bonwyn, James P. Hendrix, and K. C. Golden. *Green Jobs: A Guide to Eco-Friendly Employment* (Avon, MA: Adams Media, 2008).

McDilda, Diane Gow. *365 Ways to Live Green* (Avon, MA: Adams Media, 2008).

McKibben, Bill. *The End of Nature* (New York: Random House, 2006).

McLelland, Carol L. *Green Careers for Dummies* (Hoboken, NJ: Wiley, 2010).

Melville, Greg. *Greasy Rider: Two Dudes, One Fry-Oil-Powered Car, and a Cross-Country Search for a Greener Future* (Chapel Hill, NC: Algonquin Books of Chapel Hill, 2008).

Parks, Barbara, and Jodi Helmer. *The Complete Idiot's Guide to Green Careers* (New York: Penguin Group, 2009).

Rogers, Elizabeth, and Thomas M. Kostigen. *The Green Book* (New York: Three Rivers Press, 2007).

Rogers, Heather. *Green Gone Wrong: How Our Economy Is Undermining the Environmental Revolution* (New York: Simon & Schuster, 2010).

Savedge, Jenn. *The Green Teen Book: The Eco-Friendly Teen's Guide to Saving the Planet* (Gabriola Island, BC: New Society, 2009).

Scott, Jennifer Power. *Green Careers: You Can Make Money AND Save the Planet* (Montreal, QC: Lobster Press, 2010).

Smith, Sharon J. *The Young Activist's Guide to Building a Green Movement + Changing the World* (Berkeley, CA: Ten Speed Press, 2011).

Organizations and Their Websites

Car Talk, www.cartalk.com, includes features about cars running on biodiesel fuel and cars of the future (such as flying cars).

Defenders of Wildlife, www.defenders.org, does what its name indicates, working around the world to protect wildlife.

Earth Day Network, www.earthday.org, works in 192 countries to broaden, diversify, and mobilize the environmental movement and to promote Earth Day activities.

EcoLogo Program, www.ecologo.org, is a Canadian certification of "environmentally-preferable products."

Energy Efficiency and Renewable Energy of the U.S. Department of Energy, www.energysavers.gov.

Getgreenliving.com, www.getgreenliving.com, is a website with the latest news and articles on how to live the green life.

Humane Society of the United States, www.humanesociety.org, is a nonprofit animal protection organization.

Humane Teen, www.humaneteen.org, is part of the Humane Society and features teens who are helping animals.

National Wildlife Federation, www.nwf.org, is a conservation organization that works to protect wildlife habitat, confront global warming, and engage communities in conservation.

Natural Resources Defense Council, www.nrdc.org, is an environmental action group made up of lawyers, scientists, and other professionals.

Organic Trade Association, www.ota.com, is a business group that protects and promotes organic trade.

Treehugger, www.treehugger.com, is a media outlet dedicated to making sustainability mainstream.

U.S. Environmental Protection Agency, www.epa.gov, is responsible for protecting human health and the environment.

U.S. Fish and Wildlife Service, www.fws.gov, is a bureau within the U.S. Department of Interior that conserves, protects, and enhances fish, wildlife, and plants and their habitats.

U.S. National Park Service of the U.S. Department of Interior, www.nps.gov, is in charge of national parks, plus national monuments, battlefields, military parks, historical parks, historic sites, lakeshores, seashores, recreation areas, scenic rivers and trails, and the White House grounds.

World Wildlife Fund, www.worldwildlife.org, is a global conservation organization.

Index

About the Author

Kathlyn Gay is the author of more than 120 books that focus on social and environmental issues, culture, history, communication, and sports for a variety of audiences. A full-time freelance author, Kathlyn has also published hundreds of magazine features, stories, and plays, and she has written and contributed to encyclopedias, teachers' manuals, and textbooks. She is the author of several titles in the It Happened to Me series: *Epilepsy* (2002, with Sean McGarrahan), *Cultural Diversity* (2003), *Volunteering* (2004), *Religion and Spirituality in America* (2006), *The Military and Teens* (2008), and *Body Image and Appearance* (2009).